Low-Carb Instant Pot Cookbook

Healthy and Easy Keto Diet Pressure Cooker Recipes.

Helena Walker

Introduction

The Ketogenic diet is a must-follow diet if you want to lose weight and obtain various health benefits. For a beginner, preparing delicious keto meals can be challenging, especially when you have a busy schedule. Lose weight and save time in the kitchen with easy, set-and-forget recipes from this healthy Instant Pot Cookbook. It is not just a cookbook; it is a complete guide of Ketogenic and Instant Pot Cooking. It is a perfect companion for your daily cooking.

This book includes 100 various recipes for everyday meals and for special events. Here you will find easy breakfast recipes, tasty ideas for lunchtime and dinner, and mouthwatering desserts. These simple dump-and-forget Ketogenic Instant Pot recipes will jumpstart your Ketogenic journey, help you enter and maintain ketosis, and support your weight loss goal.

When you read this cookbook, you will find lots of knowledge that you want to know and many delicious recipes. All of these recipes are well chosen and are proven to be top recipes. All you need to do is just buy the ingredients in your local market or farmers' market and put them into the instant pot, then wait for some minutes and you will have a very nutritious and delicious dish.

Chapter 1 Eggs and Vegetables

Egg Muffins

Prep time: 5 minutes	Cook time: 10 minutes	Servings: 6

Ingredients

- Heavy cream – 2 Tbsp.
- Eggs – 4
- Salt – ¼ tsp.
- Pepper – 1/8 tsp.
- Shredded cheddar – 1/3 cup
- Water – 1 cup

Method

1. In a bowl, whisk heavy cream and eggs. Season with salt and pepper.
2. Pour mixture into 6 silicone cupcake baking molds.
3. Sprinkle cheese on top.
4. Pour water into the Instant Pot and place the steam rack.
5. Place the cupcake molds on the rack.
6. Close the lid and press Manual.

7. Cook 10 minutes and do a natural release.
8. Cool and serve.

Nutritional Facts Per Serving

- ○ Calories: 90

- ○ Fat: 6.5g

- ○ Carb: 1g

- ○ Protein: 5.8g

Mini Quiche

Prep time: 5 minutes	Cook time: 15 minutes	Servings: 1

Ingredients

- Eggs – 2
- Heavy cream – 1 Tbsp.
- Diced green pepper – 1 tbsp.
- Diced red onion – 1 Tbsp.
- Chopped fresh spinach – ¼ cup
- Salt – ½ tsp.
- Pepper – ¼ tsp.
- Water – 1 cup

Method

1. Except for the water, whisk together all the ingredients in a bowl.
2. Pour into a 4-inch ramekin.
3. Pour water into the Instant Pot and place in the steam rack.
4. Place the ramekin on the rack.
5. Close the lid and press Manual.
6. Cook 15 minutes.
7. Do a quick release and serve.

Nutritional Facts Per Serving

- Calories: 201

- Fat: 14g
- Carb: 2.5g
- Protein: 13.3g

Green Power Bowl

Prep time: 10 minutes	Cook time: 10 minutes	Servings: 1

Ingredients

- Water – 1 cup
- Eggs – 2
- Coconut oil – 1 Tbsp.
- Butter – 1 tbsp.
- Sliced almonds – 1 oz.
- Fresh spinach – 1 cup, sliced
- Kale – ½ cup, sliced
- Minced garlic – ½ clove
- Salt – ½ tsp.
- Pepper – 1/8 tsp.
- Avocado – ½, sliced
- Red pepper flakes – 1/8 tsp.

Method

1. Pour water into the Instant Pot and place steam rack.
2. Place eggs on the rack and close the lid.
3. Press Egg and cook for 6 minutes.
4. Remove the eggs, cool and peel.
5. Add a clean inner pot and press Sauté.
6. Add butter, oil, and almonds.
7. Sauté for 2 to 3 minutes until almonds soften.

8. Add salt, pepper, garlic, kale and spinach.
9. Sauté for 4 to 6 minutes and press cancel.
10. Place green in a bowl. Cut the eggs in half and add to bowl.
11. Add sliced avocado, sprinkle with red pepper flakes and serve.

Nutritional Facts Per Serving

o   Calories: 649

o   Fat: 55.2g

o   Carb: 6g

o   Protein: 21.3g

Fried Egg and Avocado Sandwich

Prep time: 5 minutes	Cook time: 15 minutes	Serving: 1

Ingredients

- Bacon – 2 slices
- Eggs – 2
- Avocado – 1, mashed

Method

1. Cook the bacon in the Instant Pot on Sauté until crisp. Remove and set aside.
2. Cook the eggs in the bacon grease and press Cancel.
3. Spread mashed avocado on one egg.
4. Place bacon on top and top with second egg.
5. Serve.

Nutritional Facts Per Serving

- Calories: 489

- Fat: 38.8g

- Carb: 2.7g

- Protein: 20

Scrambled Eggs

Prep time: 5 minutes	Cook time: 7 minutes	Servings: 4

Ingredients

- Eggs – 6
- Heavy cream – 2 Tbsp.
- Salt – 1 tsp.
- Pepper – ¼ tsp.
- Butter – 2 tbsp.
- Cream cheese – 2 oz. softened

Method

1. In a bowl, whisk the heavy cream, eggs, salt, and pepper.
2. Press Sauté and add the mixture to the Instant Pot.
3. Cook and stir until the eggs begin to firm up. Add softened cream cheese and butter.
4. Stir until eggs are cooked.
5. Serve.

Nutritional Facts Per Serving

- Calories: 232

- Fat: 18.7g

- Carb: 1.4g

- Protein: 10.5g

Southwestern Frittata

Prep time: 5 minutes	Cook time: 20 minutes	Servings: 4

Ingredients

- Coconut oil – 2 Tbsps.
- Diced onion - ¼ cup
- Diced green chilies – ¼ cup
- Green bell pepper – ½, diced
- Eggs – 8
- Salt – 1 tsp.
- Chili powder – ½ tsp.
- Garlic powder – ¼ tsp.
- Pepper – ¼ tsp.
- Heavy cream – ¼ cup
- Melted butter – 4 Tbsps.
- Shredded cheddar cheese – ½ cup
- Water – 1 cup
- Avocado – 2
- Sour cream – ¼ cup

Method

1. Melt the coconut oil on Sauté in the Instant Pot.
2. Add bell pepper, chilies, and onion.
3. Sauté for 3 minutes or until onion is translucent.

4. In a bowl, whisk butter, heavy cream, seasoning, and eggs.
5. Pour into a baking pan.
6. Press Cancel and add the pepper-onion mixture to the egg mixture.
7. Mix in cheddar and cover pan with foil.
8. Clean the inner pot and add water.
9. Place the steam rack and place the baking dish on top.
10. Close the lid and press Manual.
11. Cook for 25 minutes.
12. Do a quick release.
13. Serve with sour cream and avocado slices.

Nutritional Facts Per Serving

o   Calories: 563

o   Fat: 47.1g

o   Carb: 10.2g

o   Protein: 18.4g

Breakfast Burrito Bowl

Prep time: 10 minutes	Cook time: 15 minutes	Servings: 4

Ingredients

- Eggs – 6
- Melted butter – 3 Tbsp.
- Salt – 1 tsp.
- Pepper – ¼ tsp.
- Cooked breakfast sausage – ½ pound
- Shredded sharp cheddar cheese – ½ cup
- Salsa – ½ cup
- Sour cream – ½ cup
- Avocado – 1, cubed
- Diced green onion – ¼ cup

Method

1. Mix butter, eggs, salt, and pepper in a bowl.
2. Cook the eggs in the Instant Pot on Sauté for 5 to 7 minutes. Stir constantly.
3. When almost cooked, add the cheese, and sausage and cook until the eggs are fully cooked.
4. Press Cancel.
5. Divide eggs into bowls.
6. Top with green onion, avocado, sour cream, and salsa.
7. Serve.

Nutritional Facts Per Serving

- Calories: 613

- Fat: 49.9g

- Carb: 5.9g

- Protein: 22.9g

Green Bean Casserole

Prep time: 5 minutes	Cook time: 8 minutes	Servings: 4

Ingredients

- Butter – 4 Tbsps.
- Onion - ½, diced
- Chopped button mushrooms – ½ cup
- Chicken broth – 1 cup
- Salt – 1 tsp.
- Pepper – ¼ tsp.
- Green beans – 1 pound, trimmed
- Heavy cream – ½ cup
- Cream cheese – 1 oz.
- Xanthan gum – ¼ tsp.

Method

1. Melt the butter on Sauté in the Instant Pot.
2. Sauté mushrooms and onions for 3 minutes.
3. Add green beans, pepper, salt, and broth.

4. Close the lid and press Manual.
5. Cook 5 minutes.
6. Do a quick release and stir in the remaining ingredients.
7. Serve.

Nutritional Facts Per Serving

- Calories: 275

- Fat: 23.7g

- Carb: 7.1g

- Protein: 4g

Cabbage and Broccoli Slaw

Prep time: 5 minutes	Cook time: 10 minutes	Servings: 6

Ingredients

- Broccoli slaw – 2 cups
- Cabbage – ½ head, thinly sliced
- Chopped kale – ¼ cup
- Butter – 4 Tbsp.
- Salt – 1 tsp.
- Pepper – ¼ tsp.

Method

1. Stir-fry all the ingredients on Sauté in the Instant Pot until cabbage softens, about 7 to 10 minutes.
2. Serve.

Nutritional Facts Per Serving

- Calories: 97
- Fat: 7.2g

- o Carb: 3.8g
- o Protein: 1.9g

Garlic Mashed Cauliflower

Prep time: 3 minutes	Cook time: 1 minutes	Servings: 4

Ingredients

- o Cauliflower – 1 head, chopped into florets
- o Water – 1 cup
- o Minced garlic – 1 clove
- o Butter – 3 Tbsps.
- o Sour cream – 2 Tbsps.
- o Salt – ½ tsp.
- o Pepper – ¼ tsp.

Method

1. Add water in the Instant Pot and place the steamer rack.
2. Place cauliflower on the rack and close the lid.
3. Cook 1 minute on Steam.
4. Do a quick release.
5. Pulse the cauliflower with the remaining ingredients in a food processor.
6. Blend until creamy.
7. Serve.

Nutritional Facts Per Serving

- o   Calories: 125

- o   Fat: 9.4g

- o   Carb: 4.8g

- o   Protein: 3.1g

Cheesy Cauliflower Rice

Prep time: 3 minutes	Cook time: 1 minutes	Servings: 4

Ingredients

- Cauliflower – 1 head, chopped into florets
- Water – 1 cup
- Butter – 3 Tbsp.
- Heavy cream – 1 Tbsp.
- Shredded sharp cheddar cheese – 1 cup
- Salt – ½ tsp.
- Pepper – ¼ tsp.
- Garlic powder – ¼ tsp.

Method

1. Add water into the Instant Pot and place steamer basket.
2. Place cauliflower on top of the basket and close the lid.
3. Press Steam and cook for 1 minute.
4. Do a quick release.

5. Pulse the cauliflower in a food processor until broken into small pearls.
6. Place the cauliflower in a bowl.
7. Add remaining ingredients and gently fold.
8. Serve.

Nutritional Facts Per Serving

- Calories: 241

- Fat: 17.9g

- Carb: 5g

- Protein: 9.8g

Pesto Zucchini Noodles

Prep time: 5 minutes	Cook time: 3 minutes	Servings: 2

Ingredients

- o Zucchini – 2 large, spiralized
- o Salt – ½ tsp.
- o Pepper - ¼ tsp.
- o Butter – 2 Tbsps.
- o Pesto – ¼ cup
- o Grated Parmesan – 1/8 cup

Method

1. Season the zucchini with salt and pepper.
2. Melt the butter in the Instant Pot on Sauté.
3. Add zucchini and sauté for 2 to 3 minutes. Don't overcook.
4. Press Cancel and add pesto.
5. Sprinkle with Parmesan.
6. Serve.

Nutritional Facts Per Serving

- Calories: 182

- Fat: 23.2g

- Carb: 10g

- Protein: 7.3g

Buttery Cabbage

Prep time: 5 minutes	Cook time: 5 minutes	Servings: 4

Ingredients

- White cabbage – 1 head, sliced
- Butter – 4 Tbsp.
- Salt – ½ tsp.
- Pepper – ¼ tsp.
- Water – 1 cup

Method

1. Place butter, cabbage, salt and pepper in a bowl. Mix.
2. Pour water in the Instant Pot and place the steam rack.
3. Place the bowl on the rack.
4. Close the lid and press Manual.
5. Cook for 5 minutes.
6. Do a quick release and serve.

Nutritional Facts Per Serving

- Calories: 158
- Fat: 10g

- Carb: 7.6g

- Protein: 3g

Buttery Spinach

Prep time: 5 minutes	Cook time: 10 minutes	Servings: 2

Ingredients

- Fresh spinach – 4 cups
- Butter – 4 Tbsp.
- Salt – ½ tsp.
- Pepper – ¼ tsp.
- Garlic powder – ¼ tsp.
- Red pepper flakes – 1/8 tsp.

Method

1. Press Sauté and add all the ingredients into the Instant Pot.
2. Sauté for 10 minutes, or until greens are soft.

Nutritional Facts Per Serving

- Calories: 218
- Fat: 21.6g
- Carb: 1.3g

- Protein: 2.1g

Creamed Spinach

Prep time: 3 minutes	Cook time: 5 minutes	Servings: 6

Ingredients

- Butter – 4 Tbsps.
- Diced onion – ¼ cup
- Cream cheese – 8 oz. break into pieces
- Frozen spinach – 1 (12-oz.) bag
- Chicken broth – ½ cup
- Shredded mozzarella cheese – 1 cup

Method

1. Melt the butter on Sauté in the Instant Pot.
2. Add onion and sauté for 2 minutes.
3. Add cream cheese and press Cancel.
4. Add broth and frozen spinach.
5. Close the lid and press Manual.
6. Cook 5 minutes.
7. Do a quick release and stir in shredded mozzarella.
8. Serve.

Nutritional Facts Per Serving

- Calories: 273

- Fat: 23.9g

- Carb: 3.2g

- Protein: 8.7g

Creamy Chorizo Dip

Prep time: 5 minutes	Cook time: 10 minutes	Servings: 4

Ingredients

- o Ground chorizo – 1 pound
- o Chicken broth – 1 cup
- o Salsa – ½ cup
- o Cream cheese – 8 oz.
- o Shredded white American cheese – ½ cup

Method

1. Press Sauté and add the chorizo to the Instant Pot.
2. Cook until no longer pink and drain.
3. Add salsa and broth.
4. Place cream cheese on top of the meat.
5. Close the lid and press Manual.
6. Cook on High for 5 minutes.
7. Do a quick release and stir in the American cheese.
8. Serve.

Nutritional Facts Per Serving

- Calories: 688
- Fat: 53.1g
- Carb: 6.9g
- Protein: 28.4g

Buffalo Chicken Meatballs

Prep time: 5 minutes	Cook time: 10 minutes	Servings: 4

Ingredients

- Ground chicken – 1 pound
- Almond flour – ½ cup
- Cream cheese – 2 Tbsp.
- Dry ranch dressing mix – 1 packet
- Salt – ½ tsp.
- Pepper – ¼ tsp.
- Garlic powder – ¼ tsp.
- Water – 1 cup
- Butter – 2 Tbsp. melted
- Hot sauce – 1/3 cup
- Crumbled feta cheese – ¼ cup
- Sliced green onion – ¼ cup

Method

1. Mix flour, garlic powder, pepper, salt, ranch, cream cheese, and ground chicken in a bowl. Roll mixture into 16 balls.
2. Add 1 cup water to the Instant Pot and place a steam rack.
3. Place the meatballs on top of the steam rack and close the lid.
4. Press Meal button and cook for 10 minutes.

5. Combine hot sauce and butter in a bowl.
6. When cooked, remove the meatballs, and place in a clean bowl.
7. Toss in hot sauce mixture.
8. Top with green onions and feta and serve.

Nutritional Facts Per Serving

o   Calories: 367

o   Fat: 24.9g

o   Carb: 6.8g

o   Protein: 25g

Buffalo Chicken Dip

Prep time: 5 minutes	Cook time: 20 minutes	Servings: 6

Ingredients

- Boneless, skinless chicken breasts – 3 (6-ounce)
- Salt – ½ tsp.
- Garlic powder – ½ tsp.
- Pepper – ¼ tsp.
- Chicken broth – ¾ cup
- Buffalo sauce – ½ cup
- Cream cheese – 4 ounces, softened
- Butter – 3 Tbsp.
- Shredded cheddar cheese – 1 cup

Method

1. Rub the chicken with pepper, garlic powder, and salt.
2. Place in the Instant Pot and add buffalo sauce and broth.
3. Close the lid and press Manual. Cook 20 minutes on High.
4. Do a natural release when done.
5. Shred chicken with forks.

6. Mix in cheddar, butter, and cream cheese.

Nutritional Facts Per Serving

- o   Calories: 297

- o   Fat: 20.4g

- o   Carb: 1.2g

- o   Protein: 21.1g

Simple Meatballs

Prep time: 5 minutes	Cook time: 9 minutes	Servings: 4

Ingredients

- 85% lean ground beef – 1 pound
- Almond flour – ¼ cup
- Grated Parmesan – ¼ cup
- Egg – 1
- Dried parsley – 2 tsp.
- Salt – 1 tsp.
- Dried oregano – ½ tsp.
- Pepper – ¼ tsp.
- So, sugar added tomato sauce – 1 cup
- Beef broth – ½ cup

Method

1. Mix flour, beef, pepper, oregano, salt, parsley, egg, and parmesan in a bowl.
2. Mix well and make 12 balls.
3. Place broth and sauce into the Instant Pot.
4. Add meatballs and coat well.
5. Close the lid and press Manual.
6. Cook 9 minutes on High.
7. Do a natural release, open and serve.

Nutritional Facts Per Serving

44

- o Calories: 326
- o Fat: 23.4g
- o Carb: 7.6g
- o Protein: 26.6g

Tuna Deviled Eggs

Prep time: 10 minutes	Cook time: 8 minutes	Servings: 3

Ingredients

- Water – 1 cup
- Eggs – 6
- Tuna – 1 (5-ounce) can, drained
- Mayo – 4 Tbsp.
- Lemon juice – 1 tsp.
- Celery – 1 stalk, diced
- Dijon mustard – ¼ tsp.
- Chopped fresh dill – ¼ tsp.
- Salt – ¼ tsp.
- Garlic powder – 1/8 tsp.

Method

1. Add water to the Instant Pot and place the steamer basket.
2. Top the basket with the eggs.
3. Close and press Egg button and cook for 8 minutes.
4. In a bowl, add the remaining ingredients and mix.
5. When done, do a quick release and remove the eggs.
6. Cool the eggs and remove the shells.

7. Cut eggs in half and remove the yolks.
8. Mash the yolks with forks.
9. Add yolks to the bowl with mayo and tuna and mix well.
10. Spoon mixture into egg white halves.
11. Serve.

Nutritional Facts Per Serving

- Calories: 303

- Fat: 22.4g

- Carb: 1.3g

- Protein: 20.2g

Avocado Egg Salad

| Prep time: 10 minutes | Cook time: 8 minutes | Servings: 2 |

Ingredients

- Water – 1 cup
- Eggs – 6
- Avocado – 1, blend until smooth
- Lime juice – 2 Tbsps.
- Chili powder – ½ tsp.
- Salt – ¼ tsp.
- Mayo – 2 Tbsp.
- Chopped cilantro – 2 Tbsps.

Method

1. Add water and a steamer basket inside the Instant Pot.
2. Place the eggs on top of the basket and close the lid.
3. Press Egg and cook for 8 minutes.
4. Meanwhile, place blended avocado to a bowl.
5. Add cilantro, mayo, salt, chili powder, and lime juice to the bowl.
6. When finished, remove the eggs, cool and peel.
7. Chop the eggs into bite-sized pieces.
8. Fold chopped eggs into avocado mixture.
9. Serve.

Nutritional Facts Per Serving

- o Calories: 426

- o Fat: 32.2g

- o Carb: 3.7g

- o Protein: 20.5g

Quick Queso

Prep time: 3 minutes	Cook time: 10 minutes	Servings: 6

Ingredients

- Cream cheese – ounce, softened
- Sour cream – ½ cup
- Heavy cream – ¼ cup
- Water – 2 Tbsp.
- Shredded Monterey jack cheese - 1 cup
- Shredded pepper jack cheese – 1 cup
- 85% lean ground beef – 1 cup (mixed with ½ Tbsp. taco seasoning)

Method

1. Press Sauté and add water, heavy cream, sour cream, and cream cheese to the Instant Pot.
2. Press Cancel when the mixture starts to boil.
3. Stir in rest of the ingredients until smooth.
4. Serve with veggies.

Nutritional Facts Per Serving

- Calories: 404

- o Fat: 32g
- o Carb: 3.3g
- o Protein: 18.1g

Creamy Jalapeno Poppers

Prep time: 10 minutes	Cook time: 3 minutes	Servings: 4

Ingredients

- Jalapenos – 6 (cut lengthwise, seeds and membrane removed)
- Cream cheese – 4 ounces
- Shredded sharp cheddar cheese – ¼ cup
- Water – 1 cup
- Cooked crumbled bacon – ¼ cup

Method

1. Mix cheddar and cream cheese in a bowl.
2. Fill the jalapenos with the mixture.
3. Pour water into the Instant Pot and place a steamer basket.
4. Place the stuffed jalapenos on top of the basket.
5. Close the lid and press Manual.
6. Cook 3 minutes on High.
7. Do a quick release.
8. Serve top with crumbled bacon.

Nutritional Facts Per Serving

- o Calories: 185
- o Fat: 14.3g
- o Carb: 2.2g
- o Protein: 7.5g

Bacon Broccoli Salad

Prep time: 10 minutes	Cook time: 10 minutes	Servings: 4

Ingredients

- Bacon – 6 slices
- Fresh broccoli – 4 cups, chopped
- Mayo – ¼ cup
- Thai chili sauce – 3 Tbsps.
- Pepitas – 2 Tbsps.

Method

1. Cook bacon in the Instant Pot until crispy.
2. Remove and place on paper towel.
3. Add broccoli and stir-fry with the bacon grease for 3 minutes.
4. Press Cancel.
5. Remove broccoli and place in a bowl.
6. In another bowl, place chili sauce and mayo.
7. Add sauce mixture to the large bowl.
8. Crumble bacon over the bowl and toss.
9. Sprinkle pepitas on top to serve.
10. Serve.

Nutritional Facts Per Serving

- o   Calories: 319

- o   Fat: 26.2g

- o   Carb: 8g

- o   Protein: 7.9g

Blackened Chicken Bits and Ranch

Prep time: 5 minutes	Cook time: 15 minutes	Servings: 1

Ingredients

- Boneless, skinless chicken breast – 2 ounces, cubed
- Dried thyme – ¼ tsp.
- Paprika – ¼ tsp.
- Pepper – ¼ tsp.
- Garlic powder – ¼ tsp.
- Coconut oil – 3 Tbsp.
- Ranch dressing – ½ cup
- Hot sauce – 2 Tbsp.

Method

1. Coat chicken with the seasonings.
2. Press Sauté and heat the oil.
3. Sear chicken until thoroughly cooked.
4. Remove chicken and press Cancel.
5. Pour hot sauce and ranch into the Instant Pot.
6. Heat on Keep Warm for 5 minutes.
7. Serve chicken bites with dipping sauce.

Nutritional Facts Per Serving

- o   Calories: 228
- o   Fat: 21.4g
- o   Carb: 0.7g
- o   Protein: 6.8g

Chapter 3 Soups

Chicken Zoodle Soup

Prep time: 15 minutes	Cook time: 20 minutes	Servings: 6

Ingredients

- Celery – 3 stalks, diced
- Diced pickled jalapeno – 2 Tbsps.
- Bok choy – 1 cup, sliced into strips
- Fresh spinach – ½ cup
- Zucchini – 3, spiralized
- Coconut oil – 1 Tbsp.
- Onion – ¼, diced
- Button mushrooms – ¼ cup, diced
- Cooked diced chicken – 2 cups
- Chicken broth – 3 cups
- Bay leaf – 1
- Salt – 1 tsp.
- Garlic powder – ½ tsp.
- Cayenne pepper – 1/8 tsp.

Method

1. In a bowl, place spinach, bok choy, and jalapeno.

2. Place spiralized zucchini in another bowl.
3. Press Sauce and add the oil.
4. Add onion and mushrooms to the hot oil and sauté until onion is translucent, about 4 to 6 minutes.
5. Add spinach, bok choy, and jalapenos to the Instant Pot.
6. Cook for 4 minutes and press Cancel.
7. Add broth, bay leaf, diced chicken, and seasoning to the Instant Pot.
8. Close the lid and press Soup. Cook 20 minutes.
9. Do a natural release.
10. Add spiralized zucchini on Keep Warm mode and cook for 10 minutes.
11. Serve.

Nutritional Facts Per Serving

o   Calories: 111

o   Fat: 3.7g

o   Carb: 5g

o   Protein: 13.2g

Beef Stew

Prep time: 15 minutes	Cook time: 30 minutes	Servings: 4

Ingredients

- Coconut oil – 2 Tbsps.
- Cubed chuck roast – 1 pound
- Sliced button mushrooms -1 cup
- Onion – ½, chopped
- Beef broth – 2 cups
- Chopped celery – ½ cup
- Tomato paste – 1 Tbsp.
- Thyme – 1 tsp.
- Garlic – 2 cloves, minced
- Xanthan gum – ½ tsp.

Method

1. Heat the oil on Sauté in the Instant Pot.
2. Brown cubes of chuck roast until golden. Work in batches if necessary.
3. Add onions and mushrooms to the pot.
4. Sauté until onions are translucent. Press Cancel.
5. Add broth and deglaze the pot if needed.
6. Add garlic, thyme, tomato paste, and celery.
7. Close the lid and press Manual.
8. Cook 35 minutes on High.
9. Do a natural release.

10. Open and stir in xanthan gum.
11. Serve.

Nutritional Facts Per Serving

- Calories: 354

- Fat: 25g

- Carb: 2.9g

- Protein: 23.6g

Buffalo Chicken Soup

Prep time: 5 minutes	Cook time: 25 minutes	Servings: 4

Ingredients

- Diced onion – 2 Tbsp.
- Butter – 2 Tbsp.
- Chicken broth – 3 cups
- Boneless, skinless chicken breasts – 2 (6-ounce), cubed
- Salt – 1 tsp.
- Garlic powder – ¼ tsp.
- Pepper – ¼ tsp.
- Celery – 2 stalks, chopped
- Hot sauce – ½ cup
- Cream cheese – 4 ounces
- Shredded cheddar cheese – ½ cup
- Xanthan gum – ¼ tsp.

Method

1. Melt butter on Sauté in the Instant Pot.
2. Add onion and sauté for 2 to 3 minutes. Press Cancel.
3. Sprinkle the chicken with pepper, garlic powder, and salt.
4. Add the chicken and broth to the Instant Pot.
5. Add hot sauce and celery.
6. Place cream cheese on top of the chicken.

62

7. Close and press Manual.
8. Cook 25 minutes.
9. Do a quick release and open.
10. Add xanthan gum and cheddar.
11. Serve.

Nutritional Facts Per Serving

- Calories: 332

- Fat: 20.3g

- Carb: 2.4g

- Protein: 26.1g

Garlic Chicken Soup

Prep time: 5 minutes	Cook time: 20 minutes	Servings: 6

Ingredients

- Garlic cloves – 10, roasted and pasted
- Onion – ½, diced
- Butter – 4 Tbsp.
- Chicken broth – 4 cups
- Salt – ½ tsp.
- Pepper – ¼ tsp.
- Thyme – 1 sp.
- Boneless, skinless chicken thighs – 1 pound, cubed
- Heavy cream – ½ cup
- Cream cheese – 2 ounces

Method

1. Press Sauté and add butter, onion, and garlic to the Instant Pot.
2. Sauté for 2 to 3 minutes then press Cancel.
3. Add chicken, thyme, pepper, salt, and broth.
4. Close the lid and press Manual.
5. Cook for 20 minutes.
6. Do a quick release and stir in cream cheese and heavy cream.

7. Serve.

Nutritional Facts Per Serving

- Calories: 291

- Fat: 21.1g

- Carb: 3.5g

- Protein: 17.4g

Jalapeno Pepper Soup

Prep time: 5 minutes	Cook time: 25 minutes	Servings: 4

Ingredients

- Butter – 2 Tbsp.
- Onion – ½, diced
- Sliced pickled jalapenos – ¼ cup
- Cooked crumbled bacon – ¼ cup
- Chicken broth - 2 cups
- Cooked diced chicken – 2 cups
- Cream cheese – 4 ounces
- Salt – 1 tsp.
- Pepper – ½ tsp.
- Garlic powder – ¼ tsp.
- Heavy cream – 1/3 cup
- Shredded sharp cheddar cheese – 1 cup

Method

1. Melt butter in the Instant Pot on Sauté.
2. Add jalapenos and onion and sauté for 5 minutes.
3. Add bacon and press Cancel.

4. Add garlic, pepper, salt, cream cheese, cooked chicken and broth.
5. Close the lid and press Soup.
6. Cook for 20 minutes.
7. Do a quick release.
8. Stir in cheddar and heavy cream.
9. Serve.

Nutritional Facts Per Serving

- Calories: 524

- Fat: 35.8g

- Carb: 7.8g

- Protein: 34.9g

Creamy Mushroom Soup

Prep time: 10 minutes	Cook time: 10 minutes	Servings: 4

Ingredients

- Sliced button mushrooms – 1 pound
- Butter – 3 Tbsps.
- Diced onion – 2 Tbsps.
- Minced garlic – 2 cloves
- Chicken broth – 2 cups
- Salt – ½ tsp.
- Pepper – ¼ tsp.
- Heavy cream – ½ cup
- Xanthan gum – ¼ tsp.

Method

1. Press Sauté and add butter, mushrooms, and onion to the Instant Pot.
2. Sauté until onions and mushrooms start to brown, about 5 to 8 minutes.
3. Add garlic and sauté until fragrant. Press Cancel.
4. Add salt, pepper, and broth.

5. Close the lid and press Manual.
6. Cook for 3 minutes on High.
7. Do a quick release.
8. Stir in xanthan gum and heavy cream.
9. Serve.

Nutritional Facts Per Serving

- Calories: 219

- Fat: 19.3g

- Carb: 4.4g

- Protein: 5.2g

Cabbage Roll Soup

Prep time: 10 minutes	Cook time: 8 minutes	Servings: 4

Ingredients

- 84% lean ground pork – ½ pound
- 85% lean ground beef – ½ pound
- Diced onion - ½
- Cabbage – ½ head, thinly sliced
- Tomato paste – 2 Tbsps.
- Diced tomatoes – ½ cup
- Chicken broth – 2 cups
- Salt – 1 tsp.
- Thyme – ½ tsp.
- Garlic powder – ½ tsp.
- Pepper – ¼ tsp.

Method

1. Press Sauté and add pork and beef to Instant Pot.
2. Brown meat until no pink remains.
3. Add onions and continue to cook until soft.
4. Press Cancel and add the remaining ingredients.
5. Press Manual and cook for 8 minutes on High.
6. Do a natural release, open, and serve.

Nutritional Facts Per Serving

- o Calories: 304

- o Fat: 15.6g

- o Carb:11.8 g

- o Protein: 23.8g

Lobster Bisque

Prep time: 5 minutes	Cook time: 10 minutes	Servings: 4

Ingredients

- Butter – 4 Tbsp.
- Onion – ½, diced
- Garlic – 1 clove, minced
- Cooked lump lobster meat – 1 pound
- Salt – ½ tsp.
- Pepper – ¼ tsp.
- Paprika – ¼ tsp.
- Cayenne – 1/8 tsp.
- Tomato paste – 2 Tbsps.
- Chicken broth – 1 cup
- Seafood stock – 1 cup
- Heavy cream – ½ cup
- Xanthan gum – ½ tsp.

Method

1. Melt the butter on Sauté in the Instant Pot.
2. Add onion and sauté for 2 to 3 minutes.
3. Add garlic and sauté for 30 seconds.

72

4. Press Cancel and add broths, tomato paste, seasonings, and lobster.
5. Press Manual and cook for 7 minutes on High.
6. Do a quick release.
7. Stir in xanthan gum and heavy cream.
8. Serve. s

Nutritional Facts Per Serving

o   Calories: 338

o   Fat: 22.4g

o   Carb: 3.5g

o   Protein: 23.7g

Bacon Cheeseburger Soup

Prep time: 5 minutes	Cook time: 15 minutes	Servings: 6

Ingredients

- 85% lean ground beef – 1 pound
- Onion – ½, sliced
- Fire-roasted tomatoes – ½ (14.5 oz.) can
- Beef broth – 3 cups
- Cooked crumbled bacon – ¼ cup
- Chopped pickled jalapenos – 1 Tbsp.
- Salt – 1 tsp.
- Pepper – ½ tsp.
- Garlic powder – ½ tsp.
- Worcestershire sauce – 2 tsps.
- Cream cheese – 4 ounces
- Sharp cheddar cheese – 1 cup
- Pickle spear – 1, diced

Method

1. Brown the ground beef in the Instant Pot on Sauté.
2. Add onion and sauté until the brown is no longer pink.
3. Press Cancel.

4. Add sauce, garlic powder, pepper, salt, jalapenos, bacon, broth, and tomatoes. Stir to mix.
5. Place cream cheese on top in middle.
6. Close the lid and press Soup.
7. Cook 15 minutes on High.
8. Do a quick release.
9. Open and top with diced pickles.
10. Serve.

Nutritional Facts Per Serving

- o Calories: 358

- o Fat: 24g

- o Carb: 4.6g

- o Protein: 23.5g

Chicken and Cauliflower Soup

Prep time: 5 minutes	Cook time: 20 minutes	Servings: 4

Ingredients

- Butter – 4 Tbsp.
- Diced onion – ¼ cup
- Celery – 2 stalks, chopped
- Fresh spinach – ½ cup
- Salt – ½ tsp.
- Pepper – ¼ tsp.
- Dried thyme – ¼ tsp.
- Dried parsley – ¼ tsp.
- Bay leaf – 1
- Chicken broth – 2 cups
- Diced cooked chicken – 2 cups
- Uncooked cauliflower rice – ¾ cup
- Xanthan gum – ½ tsp.

Method

1. Melt the butter on Sauté in the Instant Pot.
2. Add onion and sauté until translucent.

3. Add spinach and celery and sauté for 2 to 3 minutes.
4. Press Cancel.
5. Add cooked chicken, broth, bay leaf, and seasoning.
6. Close the lid and press Soup.
7. Cook 10 minutes on High.
8. Do a quick release and stir in cauliflower rice.
9. Cook cauliflower on Keep Warm setting for 10 minutes.
10. Stir in xanthan gum and serve.

Nutritional Facts Per Serving

o   Calories: 228

o   Fat: 13.7g

o   Carb: 1.5g

o   Protein: 22.4g

Broccoli Cheddar Soup

Prep time: 5 minutes	Cook time: 10 minutes	Servings: 4

Ingredients

- o Butter – 2 Tbsp.
- o Onion – 1/8 cup, diced
- o Garlic powder – ½ tsp.
- o Salt – ½ tsp.
- o Pepper – ¼ tsp.
- o Chicken broth – 2 cups
- o Broccoli – 1 cup, chopped
- o Cream cheese – 1 Tbsp. softened
- o Heavy cream – ¼ cup
- o Shredded cheddar cheese – 1 cup

Method

1. Melt the butter on Sauté in the Instant Pot.
2. Add onion and sauté until translucent.
3. Press Cancel and add broccoli, broth, pepper, salt, and garlic powder to the Pot.
4. Close the lid and press Soup.
5. Cook 5 minutes on High.
6. Stir in cheddar, cream cheese, and heavy cream.

Nutritional Facts Per Serving

- ○ Calories: 249

- ○ Fat: 20.5g

- ○ Carb: 2.7g

- ○ Protein: 9g

Creamy Tuscan Soup

Prep time: 5 minutes	Cook time: 17 minutes	Servings: 4

Ingredients

- Bacon – 4 slices
- Ground Italian sausage – 1 pound
- Butter – 4 Tbsp.
- Onion – ½, diced
- Garlic – 2 cloves, minced
- Chicken broth – 3 cups
- Cream cheese – 4 ounces
- Kale – 2 cups, chopped
- Heavy cream – ½ cup
- Salt – 1 tsp.
- Pepper – ½ tsp.

Method

1. Fry the bacon in the Instant Pot on Sauté until crispy.
2. Remove and chop into pieces. Set aside.
3. Add sausage and cook until no longer pink.

4. Add butter and onion and sauté until onions are translucent.
5. Add garlic and sauté for 30 seconds. Press Cancel.
6. Add cream cheese and broth to the pot.
7. Close the lid and press Soup.
8. Cook 7 minutes on High.
9. Do a quick release and add the remaining ingredients to the pot.
10. Leave the pot on Keep Warm setting and cook for 10 minutes more.
11. Stirring occasionally.
12. Serve.

Nutritional Facts Per Serving

o Calories: 836

o Fat: 74.4g

o Carb: 5.3g

o Protein: 23.9g

Chicken Bacon Chowder

Prep time: 10 minutes	Cook time: 20 minutes	Servings: 6

Ingredients

- Bacon – ½ pound
- Salt – ½ tsp.
- Pepper – ½ tsp.
- Garlic powder – ½ tsp.
- Dried thyme – ¼ tsp.
- Boneless, skinless chicken breasts – 3 (6-oz.)
- Button mushrooms – ½ cup, sliced
- Diced medium onion – ½
- Broccoli florets – 1 cup
- Cauliflower florets – ½ cup
- Cream cheese – 4 ounces
- Chicken broth – 3 cups
- Heavy cream – ½ cup

Method

1. Cook bacon on Sauté in the Instant until fully cooked and crispy.
2. Remove from the pot, crumble and set aside.
3. Rub the chicken with thyme, garlic powder, pepper, and salt.

4. Add chicken in the Instant Pot and sear 3 to 5 minutes on each side.
5. Add broth, cauliflower, broccoli, onion, mushrooms, and cream cheese to the pot with chicken.
6. Close the lid and press Manual.
7. Cook 12 minutes on High.
8. Do a quick release.
9. Remove chicken and shred, add to the pot.
10. Stir in the heavy cream, bacon and serve.

Nutritional Facts Per Serving

o   Calories: 407

o   Fat: 28.1g

o   Carb: 3.8g

o   Protein: 26.5g

Chicken Cordon Bleu Soup

Prep time: 5 minutes	Cook time: 15 minutes	Servings: 6

Ingredients

- Boneless, skinless chicken breasts, - 2 (6-oz.) cubed
- Chicken broth – 4 cups
- Cubed ham – ½ cup
- Cream cheese – 8 ounces
- Salt – 1 tsp.
- Pepper – ½ tsp.
- Garlic powder – ½ tsp.
- Heavy cream – ½ cup
- Grated Swiss cheese – 2 cups
- Dijon mustard – 2 tsp.

Method

1. Except for mustard, cream cheese, and heavy cream, place all ingredients into Instant Pot.
2. Close the lid and press Soup.
3. Cook 15 minutes on High.
4. Do a quick release and stir in mustard, cheese, and heavy cream.

5. Serve.

Nutritional Facts Per Serving

- o   Calories: 439

- o   Fat: 30.2g

- o   Carb: 4.7g

- o   Protein: 28.9g

Creamy Enchilada Soup

Prep time: 10 minutes	Cook time: 40 minutes	Servings: 6

Ingredients

- Boneless, skinless chicken breasts – 2 (6-oz.)
- Chili powder – ½ Tbsp.
- Salt – ½ tsp.
- Garlic powder – ½ tsp.
- Pepper – ¼ tsp.
- Red enchilada sauce – ½ cup
- Onion – ½ diced
- Green chilies – 1 (4-oz.) can
- Chicken broth – 2 cups
- Pickled jalapenos – 1/8 cup
- Cream cheese – 4 ounces
- Uncooked cauliflower rice – 1 cup
- Diced avocado – 1
- Shredded mild cheddar cheese – 1 cup
- Sour cream – ½ cup

Method

1. Rub the chicken with seasoning and set aside.
2. Add enchilada sauce into the Instant Pot and add chicken on top.
3. Add jalapenos, broth, chilies, and onion.

86

4. Place cream cheese on top of the chicken.
5. Close the lid and cook 25 minutes on High.
6. When done, do a quick release and shred the chicken with forks.
7. Mix and add cauliflower rice. Cover.
8. Cook the cauliflower on Keep Warm setting for 15 minutes.
9. Serve with sour cream, cheddar, and avocado.

Nutritional Facts Per Serving

- Calories: 318

- Fat: 18.9g

- Carb: 6.7g

- Protein: 20.7g

Chapter 4 Poultry

Salsa Verde Chicken

Prep time: 5 minutes	Cook time: 12 minutes	Servings: 4

Ingredients

- o Salt – 1 tsp.
- o Chili powder – 1 tsp.
- o Garlic powder – ½ tsp.
- o Chicken breasts – 2 (6-ounce) boneless, skinless
- o Coconut oil – 1 Tbsp.
- o Chicken broth – ¼ cup
- o Salsa Verde – 1 cup
- o Butter – 2 Tbsp.

Method

1. In a bowl, mix all the seasoning and rub the chicken with it.
2. Press the Sauté and add coconut oil.
3. Place the chicken and sear 3 to 4 minutes on each side.

4. Add salsa verde and chicken broth.
5. Close the lid and press Manual. Cook 12 minutes on High.
6. Do a natural release and open the lid.
7. Remove the chicken and shred with forks.
8. Return chicken to the warm pot and add butter.
9. Allow to melt for 10 minutes.
10. Serve warm with toppings.

Nutritional Facts Per Serving

- Calories: 185

- Fat: 13.4g

- Carb: 2.8g

- Protein: 20.2g

Ranch Chicken

Prep time: 5 minutes	Cook time: 20 minutes	Servings: 6

Ingredients

- Salt – 1 tsp.
- Pepper – ¼ tsp.
- Dried oregano – ¼ tsp.
- Garlic powder – ½ tsp.
- Skinless chicken breasts – 3 (6-ounce)
- Chicken broth – 1 cup
- Dry ranch – 1 packet
- Cream cheese – 8 ounces
- Butter – 1 stick

Method

1. In a bowl, mix the seasoning and rub the chicken with it.
2. Place the chicken into the Instant Pot and add broth.
3. Place butter and cream cheese on top of the chicken.
4. Close the lid and cook for 20 minutes on High.
5. Do a natural release.

6. Remove chicken and shred with forks.
7. Return to Instant Pot and serve.

Nutritional Facts Per Serving

- Calories: 383

- Fat: 26.9g

- Carb: 4.5g

- Protein: 21.9g

Lemon Herb Whole Chicken

Prep time: 5 minutes	Cook time: 25 minutes	Servings: 4

Ingredients

- Salt – 3 tsp.
- Garlic powder – 3 tsp.
- Dried rosemary – 2 tsp.
- Dried parsley – 2 tsp.
- Pepper – 1 tsp.
- Whole chicken – 1 (5 pound)
- Coconut oil – 2 Tbsp.
- Chicken Broth – 1 cup
- Lemon – 1, zested and quartered

Method

1. In a bowl, mix pepper, parsley, rosemary, garlic, and salt.
2. Rub the chicken with the mixture.
3. Press Sauté and add oil to the Instant Pot.
4. Add chicken and brown for 5 to 7 minutes.
5. Press Cancel and remove the chicken.
6. Add broth and deglaze the pot.
7. Place lemon quarters inside the chicken and sprinkle the chicken with lemon zest.

8. Place chicken back into the pot.
9. Close the lid and press Meat.
10. Cook on High for 25 minutes.
11. Do a natural release when done.
12. Slice the chicken and serve.

Nutritional Facts Per Serving

- Calories: 861

- Fat: 62.9g

- Carb: 2.1g

- Protein: 45.5g

Chicken Casserole

Prep time: 15 minutes	Cook time: 15 minutes	Servings: 4

Ingredients

- o   Broccoli florets – 1 cup
- o   Fresh spinach – ½ cup
- o   Whole-milk ricotta – ¼ cup
- o   Alfredo sauce – 1 ½ cups
- o   Salt – ½ tsp.
- o   Pepper – ¼ tsp.
- o   Thin-sliced deli chicken – 1 pound
- o   Whole-milk mozzarella cheese – 1 cup , shredded
- o   Water – 1 cup

Method

1. Place broccoli in a bowl.
2. Add salt, pepper, sauce, ricotta, and spinach and mix.
3. Separate into three sections with a spoon.
4. Layer chicken in a bowl.
5. Top the chicken with veggie mix.
6. Then top veggie with mozzarella.

7. Repeat until all veggie mix is used.
8. Finish casserole with mozzarella.
9. Cover the dish with foil.
10. Pour water into the Instant Pot.
11. Place steamer rack in the pot.
12. Place the dish on top of the rack.
13. Close the lid and press Manual.
14. Cook on High for 15 minutes.
15. Do a quick release and remove.
16. You can broil in the oven for a few minutes to make the top golden.

Nutritional Facts Per Serving

o   Calories: 283

o   Fat: 13.3g

o   Carb: 9.1g

o   Protein: 29.3g

Sweet and Sour Meatballs

Prep time: 10 minutes	Cook time: 10 minutes	Servings: 4

Ingredients

- Ground chicken – 1 pound
- Egg – 1
- Salt – 1 tsp.
- Pepper – 1 tsp.
- Garlic powder – 1 tsp.
- Diced onion – ½
- Water – 1
- Erythritol – 2 tsp.
- Rice vinegar – 1 tsp.
- No sugar added ketchup – 2 tsp.
- Sriracha – ½ tsp.

Method

1. In a bowl, mix onion, garlic powder, salt, pepper, egg, and chicken.
2. Make small balls with the mixture.
3. Add water to the Instant Pot.
4. Place meatballs on the steam rack.

5. Close the lid and press Manual.
6. Cook 10 minutes on High.
7. In a bowl, mix sriracha, ketchup, vinegar, and erythritol.
8. When finished, do a quick release.
9. Toss meatballs in the sauce.
10. Serve.

Nutritional Facts Per Serving

- Calories: 152

- Fat: 7.6g

- Carb: 1.7g

- Protein: 17.4g

Pesto Chicken

Prep time: 5 minutes	Cook time: 20 minutes	Servings: 2

Ingredients

- Boneless, skinless chicken breasts – 2 (6-oz.) butterflied
- Salt – ½ tsp.
- Pepper – ¼ tsp.
- Garlic powder – ¼ tsp.
- Dried parsley – ¼ tsp.
- Coconut oil – 2 Tbsp.
- Water – 1 cup
- Whole-milk ricotta – ¼ cup
- Pesto – ¼ cup
- Shredded whole-milk mozzarella cheese – ¼ cup
- Chopped parsley for garnish

Method

1. Rub the chicken with seasonings.
2. Melt the oil in the instant Pot on Sauté.

3. Add chicken and sauté for 3 to 5 minutes.
4. Remove chicken and place in a bowl.
5. Pour water into the pot and deglaze.
6. Add the ricotta onto the chicken.
7. Pour pesto and drizzle with mozzarella.
8. Cover the dish with foil.
9. Place a steam rack into the Instant Pot and place the foil covered dish on top.
10. Cover with the lid and press Manual.
11. Cook 20 minutes on High.
12. Do a natural release when done.
13. Serve.

Nutritional Facts Per Serving

- Calories: 518

- Fat: 31.8g

- Carb: 3.6g

- Protein: 46.5g

Chicken Piccata

Prep time: 5 minutes	Cook time: 20 minutes	Servings: 4

Ingredients

- Boneless, skinless chicken breasts – 4 (6-oz.)
- Salt – ½ tsp.
- Pepper – ¼ tsp.
- Garlic powder – ½ tsp.
- Coconut oil – 2 Tbsp.
- Water – 1 cup
- Butter – 4 Tbsp.
- Juice of 1 lemon
- Capers – 2 Tbsp.
- Garlic – 2 cloves, minced
- Xanthan gum – ¼ tsp.

Method

1. Rub the chicken with garlic powder, pepper, and salt.
2. Melt the oil on Sauté in the Instant Pot.
3. Sear the chicken until golden on each side.
4. Remove chicken and add water to deglaze the pot.
5. Place the steam rack and add the chicken.
6. Close the lid and press Manual.
7. Cook for 10 minutes on High.
8. Do a natural release when done.
9. Remove chicken and set aside.

10. Strain the broth into a bowl and then return to the Instant Pot.
11. Press Sauté and add, butter, xanthan gum, garlic, capers, and lemon juice.
12. Stir continuously until the sauce thickens, about 5 minutes.
13. Serve over chicken.

Nutritional Facts Per Serving

- ○ Calories: 337

- ○ Fat: 19.5g

- ○ Carb: 1.4g

- ○ Protein: 32.3g

Garlic Parmesan Drumsticks

Prep time: 5 minutes	Cook time: 15 minutes	Servings: 4

Ingredients

- Chicken drumsticks – 2 pounds (about 8 pieces)
- Salt – 1 tsp.
- Pepper – ¼ tsp.
- Garlic powder – ½ tsp.
- Dried parsley – 1 tsp.
- Dried oregano – ½ tsp.
- Water – 1 cup
- Butter – 1 stick
- Chicken broth – ½ cup
- Grated Parmesan cheese – ½ cup
- Cream cheese – 2 ounces, softened
- Heavy cream – ¼ cup
- Pepper – 1/8 tsp.

Method

1. Rub the drumsticks with the seasoning.
2. Pour water into the Instant Pot and place steam rack.
3. Place drumsticks on top and close the lid.

4. Press Manual and cook 15 minutes on High.
5. Do a natural release and open.
6. If you want crispy skin, then broil the chicken in a preheated oven for 3 to 5 minutes per side.
7. Meanwhile, pour water into the Instant Pot and press Sauté.
8. Melt the butter and add pepper, heavy cream, cream cheese, Parmesan, and broth.
9. Whisk to mix.
10. Pour the sauce over drumsticks.
11. Garnish with parsley and serve.

Nutritional Facts Per Serving

o   Calories: 786

o   Fat: 55.4g

o   Carb:3.4g

o   Protein: 53.3g

Chicken Enchilada Bowl

Prep time: 10 minutes	Cook time: 25 minutes	Servings: 4

Ingredients

- Boneless, skinless chicken breasts – 2 (6-ounce)
- Salt – ½ tsp.
- Garlic powder – ½ tsp.
- Pepper – ¼ tsp.
- Chili powder – 2 tsp.
- Coconut oil – 2 Tbsp.
- Red enchilada sauce – ¾ cup
- Chicken broth – ¼ cup
- Diced onion – ¼ cup
- Green chilies -1 (4-ounce) can
- Cooked cauliflower rice – 2 cups
- Diced avocado – 1
- Sour cream – ½ cup
- Shredded cheddar cheese – 1 cup

Method

1. Rub chicken with chili powder, pepper, garlic powder, and salt.

2. Press Sauté and melt the oil into the Instant Pot.
3. Sear the chicken on both sides and press Cancel.
4. Add broth and sauce.
5. Add chilies and onions to the pot and close the lid.
6. Press Manual and cook 25 minutes on High.
7. Do a quick release and shred chicken.
8. Serve chicken over cauliflower rice top with cheddar, sour cream, and avocado.

Nutritional Facts Per Serving

- Calories: 425

- Fat: 26g

- Carb: 7.1g

- Protein: 29.4g

Turkey Tomato Meatballs

Prep time: 10 minutes	Cook time: 10 minutes	Servings: 4

Ingredients

- Almond flour – 1/3 cup
- Diced tomatoes – 3 ½ cups
- Basil – 1 tsp.
- Ground turkey – 1 pound
- Chicken stock – ¼ cup
- Onion – ¼, diced
- Minced garlic – 1 tsp.
- Italian seasoning – 1 tsp.
- Salt and black pepper to taste

Method

1. In a bowl, place the flour, onion, basil, and turkey. Season with salt and pepper.
2. Mix and make meatballs.
3. Add the meatballs and other ingredients into the Instant Pot and stir to mix well.
4. Close the lid and press Manual.

5. Cook 10 minutes on High.
6. Do a quick release when done.
7. Open the lid and serve.

Nutritional Facts Per Serving

- o   Calories: 326

- o   Fat: 14g

- o   Carb: 4g

- o   Protein: 27g

Cauliflower Turkey Salsa

Prep time: 10 minutes	Cook time: 15 minutes	Servings: 5

Ingredients

- Cooked and shredded turkey – 2 cups
- Cream cheese – 4 ounces
- Cauliflower florets – 2 ½ cups, chopped
- Shredded cheddar cheese – 1 cup
- Sour cream – ¼ cup
- Salsa verde – ½ cup
- Salt and ground black pepper to taste
- Water – 1 ½ cups

Method

1. Add water to the Instant Pot.
2. Grease a steamer basket with oil and place in the pot.
3. Arrange the ingredients over the basket and mix.
4. Close the lid and press Manual.
5. Cook 15 minutes on High.
6. Do a quick release when done.

7. Open the lid and serve.

Nutritional Facts Per Serving

- o Calories: 324

- o Fat: 18g

- o Carb: 5g

- o Protein: 34g

Barbecue Wings

Prep time: 5 minutes	Cook time: 12 minutes	Servings: 4

Ingredients

- Chicken wings - 1 pound
- Salt – 1 tsp.
- Pepper - ½ tsp.
- Garlic powder – ¼ tsp.
- Sugar-free barbecue sauce – 1 cup, divided
- Water – 1 cup

Method

1. In a bowl, mix wings, half of the sauce, garlic powder, salt, and pepper.
2. Add water into the Instant Pot and place a steam rack.
3. Place wings on the steam rack and close the lid.
4. Press Manual and cook 12 minutes on High.
5. Do a quick release, remove and toss in remaining sauce.
6. If you want crispier wings, then broil the wings for 5 to 7 minutes in the oven.

Nutritional Facts Per Serving

- Calories: 237

- o Fat: 14.9g
- o Carb: 4.2g
- o Protein: 19.9g

Jamaican Curry Chicken

Prep time: 5 minutes	Cook time: 20 minutes	Servings: 4

Ingredients

- Chicken drumsticks – 1 ½ pound
- Salt – 1 tsp.
- Jamaican curry powder – 1 Tbsp.
- Onion – ½, diced
- Dried thyme – ½ tsp.
- Chicken broth – 1 cup

Method

1. Rub the drumsticks with salt and curry powder.
2. Place rest of the ingredients and chicken into the Instant Pot.
3. Press Manual and cook 20 minutes on High.
4. Do a natural release and serve.

Nutritional Facts Per Serving

- Calories: 284

- Fat: 14.11g

- Carb: 1.4g

- Protein: 31.3g

Chicken Parmesan

Prep time: 5 minutes	Cook time: 15 minutes	Servings: 2

Ingredients

- Coconut oil – 2 Tbsp.
- Salt – ½ tsp.
- Pepper – ¼ tsp.
- Dried basil – ¼ tsp.
- Garlic powder – ½ tsp.
- Dried parsley – ¼ tsp.
- Boneless, skinless chicken breasts – 2 (6-ounce), butterflied
- Water – ½ cup
- No sugar added tomato sauce – 1 cup
- Grated Parmesan cheese – ¼ cup
- Shredded whole-milk mozzarella cheese – ¼ cup

Method

1. Melt the oil in the Instant Pot on Sauté.
2. Rub the chicken with seasoning and sear 4 minutes on each side.
3. Add tomato sauce and water and close the lid.
4. Press Manual and cook 15 minutes on High.
5. When finished, do a quick release and open.

6. Add mozzarella and Parmesan and place the lid.
7. Keep the pot on Keep Warm mode for 5 minutes.
8. Top with parsley and serve.

Nutritional Facts Per Serving

- o Calories: 548

- o Fat: 28.7g

- o Carb: 8.4g

- o Protein: 48.9g

Italian Chicken Thighs

Prep time: 10 minutes	Cook time: 15 minutes	Servings: 4

Ingredients

- Chicken thighs – 4 (bone-in)
- Garlic – 2 cloves, minced
- Salt – 1 tsp.
- Pepper – ¼ tsp.
- Dried basil – ¼ tsp.
- Dried parsley – ¼ tsp.
- Dried oregano – ½ tsp.
- Water – 1 cup

Method

1. Place chicken in a bowl.
2. Rub the chicken with all the spices, herbs, and seasoning.
3. Add water to the Instant Pot and place steam rack.
4. Place chicken thighs on the steam rack and close the lid.
5. Press Manual and cook 15 minutes on High.
6. Do a quick release and remove.
7. Broil chicken in the oven for 3 to 5 minutes if you want crispy chicken.

Nutritional Facts Per Serving

- ○ Calories: 429

- ○ Fat: 28.8g

- ○ Carb: 1g

- ○ Protein: 32g

Chapter 5 Beef and Pork

Spicy Brisket

Prep time: 5 minutes	Cook time:110 minutes	Servings: 6

Ingredients

- Salt – 3 tsp.
- Pepper – 2 tsp.
- Garlic powder – 1 tsp.
- Dried thyme – 1 tsp.
- Dried rosemary – ½ tsp.
- Beef brisket – 1 (5-pound)
- Avocado oil – 1 Tbsp.
- Beef broth – 1 cup
- Pickled jalapeno juice – ½ cup
- Pickled jalapenos – ½ cup
- Onion – ½, chopped

Method

1. In a bowl, combine rosemary, thyme, garlic powder, pepper, and salt.
2. Rub the brisket with the mixture and set aside.
3. Warm the avocado oil over Sauté in the Instant Pot.
4. Sear each side of brisket for 5 minutes.

5. Add onions, jalapenos, jalapeno juice, and broth to the Instant Pot.
6. Close the lid and press Manual.
7. Cook for 100 minutes.
8. Do a natural release for 30 to 40 minutes. Avoid quick release.
9. Remove brisket, and slice.
10. Pour with the strained broth and serve.

Nutritional Facts Per Serving

- Calories: 1,001

- Fat: 68.3g

- Carb: 8.2g

- Protein: 62g

Lime Pulled Pork

Prep time: 5 minutes	Cook time: 30 minutes	Servings: 4

Ingredients

- Chili adobo sauce – 1 Tbsp.
- Chili powder – 1 Tbsp.
- Salt – 2 tsp.
- Garlic powder – 1 tsp.
- Cumin – 1 tsp.
- Pepper – ½ tsp.
- Cubed pork butt – 1 (2 ½ to 3) pound
- Coconut oil – 1 Tbsp.
- Beef broth – 2 cups
- Lime – 1, cut into wedges
- Chopped cilantro – ¼ cup

Method

1. In a bowl, mix pepper, cumin, garlic powder, salt, chili powder, and sauce.
2. Melt the oil on Sauté in the Instant Pot.
3. Rub the pork with spice mixture.
4. Place pork and sear for 3 to 5 minutes per side.
5. Add broth and close the lid.
6. Press Manual and cook 30 minutes.

7. Do a natural release and open.
8. Shred pork.
9. If you want crispy pork, then heat in a skillet until the pork is crisp.
10. Serve warm with cilantro garnish and fresh lime wedges.

Nutritional Facts Per Serving

o   Calories: 570

o   Fat: 35g

o   Carb: 2g

o   Protein: 55g

Chipotle Pork Chops

Prep time: 7 minutes	Cook time: 15 minutes	Servings: 4

Ingredients

- Coconut oil – 2 Tbsp.
- Chipotle chilies – 3
- Adobo sauce – 2 Tbsp.
- Cumin – 2 tsp.
- Dried thyme – 1 tsp.
- Salt – 1 tsp.
- Boneless pork chops – 4 (5-ounce)
- Onion – ½, chopped
- Bay leaves – 2
- Chicken broth – 1 cup
- Fire-roasted diced tomatoes – ½ (7-ounce) can
- Chopped cilantro – 1/3 cup

Method

1. Melt the oil on Sauté in the Instant Pot.
2. In a food processor, add salt, thyme, cumin, sauce, and chilies. Pulse to make a paste.
3. Rub paste into the pork chops.
4. Sear the chops 5 minutes on each side.

5. Add cilantro, tomatoes, broth, bay leaves, and onion to the Instant Pot.
6. Close the lid and press Manual.
7. Cook 15 minutes on High.
8. Do a natural release when done.
9. Serve warm with cilantro garnish.

Nutritional Facts Per Serving

o   Calories: 375

o   Fat: 24.2g

o   Carb: 3.4g

o   Protein: 31.3g

Buttery Pot Roast

Prep time: 5 minutes	Cook time: 90 minutes	Servings: 4

Ingredients

- Onion powder – 4 tsp.
- Dried parsley – 2 tsp.
- Salt – 1 tsp.
- Garlic powder – 1 tsp.
- Dried oregano – ½ tsp.
- Pepper – ½ tsp.
- Chuck roast – 1 (2-pound)
- Coconut oil – 1 Tbsp.
- Beef broth – 1 cup
- Dry ranch seasoning – ½ packet
- Butter – 1 stick
- Pepperoncini – 10

Method

1. Press Sauté and heat the Pot.
2. In a bowl, mix pepper, oregano, garlic powder, salt, parsley, and onion powder.
3. Rub seasoning onto the roast.

124

4. Add oil the pot and place roast.
5. Sear 5 minutes on each side.
6. Remove roast and set aside.
7. Add broth and deglaze.
8. Place roast back into the Instant Pot.
9. Sprinkle with ranch powder.
10. Place butter on top and add pepperoncini.
11. Close the lid and press Manual.
12. Cook 90 minutes.
13. Do a natural release.
14. Remove lid and remove roast.
15. Slice and serve.

Nutritional Facts Per Serving

- Calories: 561

- Fat: 32.9g

- Carb: 5.1g

- Protein: 51.2g

Creamy Mushroom Pot Roast

Prep time: 10 minutes	Cook time: 90 minutes	Servings:6

Ingredients

- Button mushrooms – 1 cup, sliced
- Onion – ½ cup, sliced
- Coconut oil – 1 Tbsp.
- Dried minced onion – 2 Tbsps.
- Dried parsley – 2 tsps.
- Pepper – 1 tsp.
- Garlic powder – 1 tsp.
- Dried oregano – ½ tsp.
- Salt – 1 tsp.
- Chuck roast – 1 (2 to 3 pounds)
- Beef broth – 1 cup
- Butter – 4 Tbsps.
- Cream cheese – 2 oz.
- Heavy cream – ¼ cup

Method

1. Press the Sauté and add oil, onion, and mushrooms to the Instant Pot.
2. Stir-fry for 5 minutes.

126

3. In a bowl, mix salt, oregano, garlic, pepper, parsley, and minced onion and rub into the chuck roast.
4. Press Cancel and add the roast and broth into the pot.
5. Place butter and cream cheese on top.
6. Close the lid and press Meal.
7. Cook for 90 minutes.
8. Do a natural release when done.
9. Stir in heavy cream.
10. Remove roast and press Sauté.
11. Reduce sauce for 10 minutes.
12. Serve roast with the sauce.

Nutritional Facts Per Serving

- Calories: 413

- Fat: 22.4g

- Carb: 2.5g

- Protein: 43.5g

Salisbury Steak in Mushroom Sauce

Prep time: 10 minutes	Cook time: 15 minutes	Servings: 4

Ingredients

- 85% lean ground beef – 1 pound
- Steak seasoning – 1 tsp.
- Egg – 1
- Butter – 2 Tbsp.
- Onion – ½, sliced
- Sliced button mushrooms – ½ cup
- Beef broth – 1 cup
- Cream cheese – 2 oz.
- Heavy cream – ¼ cup
- Xanthan gum – ¼ tsp.

Method

1. Mix egg, steak seasoning, and ground beef in a bowl. Make 4 patties and set aside.
2. Press Sauté and melt the butter.
3. Add mushrooms and onion and stir-fry for 3 to 5 minutes.
4. Press Cancel and add beef patties, broth, and cream cheese to the Instant Pot.
5. Close the lid and press Manual.

6. Cook 15 minutes on High.
7. Do a natural release when done.
8. Remove the patties and set aside.
9. Add xanthan gum and heavy cream. Whisk to mix.
10. Reduce the sauce on Sauté for 5 to 10 minutes.
11. Press Cancel and add patties back to the Instant Pot.
12. Serve.

Nutritional Facts Per Serving

- Calories: 420

- Fat: 30.5g

- Carb: 2.4g

- Protein: 24.6g

Brisket with Cauliflower

Prep time: 5 minutes	Cook time: 15 minutes	Servings: 4

Ingredients

- Water – 1 cup
- Fresh cauliflower – 2 cups, chopped
- Butter – 3 Tbsps.
- Onion – ¼, diced
- Pickled jalapeno slices – ¼ cup
- Cooked brisket – 2 cups
- Cream cheese – 2 oz. softened
- Shredded sharp cheddar cheese – 1 cup
- Heavy cream – ¼ cup
- Cooked crumbled bacon – ¼ cup
- Sliced green onions – 2 Tbsps.

Method

1. Add water to the Instant Pot.
2. Steam the cauliflower on a steamer basket for 1 minute.
3. Do a quick release and set aside.
4. Pour out water and Press Sauté.
5. Add butter, jalapeno slices, and onion.

6. Sauté for 4 minutes, add cream cheese and cooked brisket.
7. Cook 2 minutes more.
8. Add cauliflower, heavy cream, and sharp cheddar.
9. Press Cancel and gently mix until mixed well.
10. Sprinkle with green onions, and crumbled bacon.
11. Serve.

Nutritional Facts Per Serving

- Calories: 574

- Fat: 40.4g

- Carb: 7.9g

- Protein: 32.7g

Pork Chops in Mushroom Gravy

Prep time: 5 minutes	Cook time: 15 minutes	Servings: 4

Ingredients

- Pork chops – 4 (5-ounce)
- Salt – 1 tsp.
- Pepper – ½ tsp.
- Avocado oil – 2 Tbsps.
- Button mushrooms – 1 cup, chopped
- Onion – ½, sliced
- Minced garlic – 1 clove
- Chicken broth – 1 cup
- Heavy cream – ¼ cup
- Butter – 4 Tbsps.
- Xanthan gum – ¼ tsp.
- Chopped fresh parsley - 1 Tbsp.

Method

1. Rub the pork chops with salt and pepper.
2. Heat the avocado oil in the Instant Pot and Sauté.
3. Add mushroom and sauté for 3 to 5 minutes.
4. Add pork chops and onion and sauté for 3 minutes.
5. Add broth and garlic and close the lid.
6. Press Manual and cook 15 minutes on High.
7. Do a natural release.
8. Remove lid and place pork chops on a plate.

9. Press Sauté and add xanthan gum, butter, and heavy cream.
10. Reduce the sauce for 5 to 10 minutes.
11. Add pork chops back into the pot.
12. Serve chops topped with parsley and sauce.

Nutritional Facts Per Serving

- o Calories: 516

- o Fat: 39.7g

- o Carb: 2.3g

- o Protein: 31.6g

Beef and Spaghetti Squash Casserole

Prep time: 10 minutes	Cook time: 20 minutes	Servings: 4

Ingredients

- Spaghetti squash – 6 pounds, cooked and scraped out into long strands with a fork
- No sugar added tomato sauce – 1 cup
- Whole-milk ricotta – ½ cup
- Grated parmesan cheese – ¼ cup
- Butter – 3 Tbsps.
- Dried parsley – ½ tsp.
- Garlic powder – ½ tsp.
- Dried basil – ¼ tsp.
- Salt – ½ tsp.
- Pepper – ¼ tsp.
- 85% lean ground beef – 1 pound, cooked
- Shredded mozzarella cheese – 1 cup, divided
- Water – 1 cup

Method

1. Place the squash into a bowl.

134

2. Add remaining ingredients except for water (reserve ½ mozzarella).
3. Mix and pour mixture into a bowl.
4. Sprinkle remaining cheese on top and cover with a foil.
5. Pour water into the Instant Pot and place steam rack.
6. Place bowl on the steam rack and close the lid.
7. Press Manual and cook for 10 minutes.
8. Do a natural release.
9. You can broil the dish in the oven for a few minutes to brown the top.
10. Serve.

Nutritional Facts Per Serving

- Calories: 628

- Fat: 37.5g

- Carb: 9g

- Protein: 36.5g

Mini BBQ Meatloaf

Prep time: 5 minutes	Cook time: 25 minutes	Servings: 4

Ingredients

- o   85% lean ground beef – 1 pound
- o   Onion – ½, diced
- o   Green pepper – ½, diced
- o   Almond flour – ¼ cup
- o   Shredded mozzarella cheese – ¼ cup
- o   Egg - 1
- o   Salt – 1 tsp.
- o   Pepper – ¼ tsp.
- o   Garlic powder – 1 tsp.
- o   No sugar added barbecue sauce – ¼ cup

Method

1. Except for the barbecue sauce, mix all ingredients in a bowl.
2. Make two loaves and place into loaf pans.
3. Pour sauce on top and cover with foil.
4. Pour 1 cup water into the Instant Pot and place the steam rack.

5. Place the meatloaf pans on steam rack.
6. Close the lid and press Manual.
7. Cook 25 minutes on High.
8. Serve.

Nutritional Facts Per Serving

o   Calories: 340

o   Fat: 20.3g

o   Carb: 4.2g

o   Protein: 26.4g

BBQ Ribs

Prep time: 5 minutes	Cook time: 50 minutes	Servings: 4

Ingredients

- Ribs – 1 (4-pound) rack
- Chili powder – 1 Tbsp.
- Salt – 1 tsp.
- Dried parsley – 1 tsp.
- Pepper – ½ tsp.
- Garlic powder – ½ tsp.
- Onion powder – ½ tsp.
- No sugar added barbecue sauce – ½ cup
- Water – 1 cup
- Liquid smoke – 1 Tbsp.

Method

1. Rub ribs with half barbecue sauce and seasonings.
2. Pour water, and liquid smoke into the Instant Pot and place a steam rack.
3. Place rack on the steam rack and close the lid.
4. Press Meat and cook 50 minutes on High.
5. When done, place ribs on foil-lined baking sheet.

6. Brush with remaining sauce and serve.
7. If you want a caramelized sauce, then broil it in the oven for a few minutes.

Nutritional Facts Per Serving

- o Calories: 421

- o Fat: 23.6g

- o Carb: 3.5g

- o Protein: 39.5g

Cheesy Beef and Broccoli

Prep time: 5 minutes	Cook time: 10 minutes	Servings: 4

Ingredients

- 85% lean ground beef – 1 pound
- Salt – 1 tsp.
- Garlic powder – ½ tsp.
- Dried parsley – ½ tsp.
- Dried oregano – ¼ tsp.
- Butter – 2 Tbsp.
- Beef broth – ¾ cup
- Broccoli florets – 2 cups
- Heavy cream – ¼ cup
- Shredded cheddar cheese – 1 cup

Method

1. Brown the beef on Sauté in the Instant Pot.
2. Press Cancel and sprinkle seasonings over meat.
3. Add broccoli, broth, and butter. Close the lid.
4. Press Manual and cook for 2 minutes on High.
5. When done, press Cancel and stir in cheddar and heavy cream.
6. Serve.

Nutritional Facts Per Serving

140

- o Calories: 476
- o Fat: 33.5g
- o Carb: 3g
- o Protein: 29.9g

Pizza Casserole

Prep time: 10 minutes	Cook time: 15 minutes	Servings: 4

Ingredients

- o   Italian Sausage – ½ pound
- o   Diced onion – ¼ cup
- o   Diced green pepper – ¼ cup
- o   Cooked bacon crumbles – ¼ cup
- o   Pepperoni – 16 slices
- o   Shredded mozzarella cheese – 2 cups
- o   Fresh spinach – 2 cups
- o   No sugar added tomato sauce – 1 ½ cup
- o   Grated Parmesan cheese – ½ cup

Method

1. Brown the sausage on Sauté in the Instant Pot.
2. Add bacon crumbles, pepper, and onion.
3. Cook until onion softens.
4. Add the remaining ingredients, except for the Parmesan.
5. Sprinkle with Parmesan and serve.

Nutritional Facts Per Serving

- o   Calories: 616

- o Fat: 43.4g

- o Carb: 8g

- o Protein: 33.3g

Taco Cabbage Casserole

Prep time: 5 minutes	Cook time: 4 minutes	Servings: 4

Ingredients

- 85% Lean ground beef – 1 pound
- Shredded white cabbage – 2 cups
- Salsa – 1 cup
- Salt – 1 tsp.
- Chili powder – 1 Tbsp.
- Cumin – ½ tsp.
- Water – ½ cup
- Shredded cheddar cheese – 1 cup

Method

1. Brown the beef on Sauté in the Instant Pot.
2. Then add remaining ingredients, except for cheese.
3. Close the lid and press Manual.
4. Cook 4 minutes on High.
5. Do a quick release and stir in cheddar.
6. Serve.

Nutritional Facts Per Serving

- Calories: 393
- Fat: 23g
- Carb: 5.1g
- Protein: 29.5g

Butter Beef and Spinach

Prep time: 2 minutes	Cook time: 10 minutes	Servings: 4

Ingredients

- 85% lean ground beef – 1 pound
- Water – 1 cup
- Fresh spinach – 4 cups
- Salt – ¾ tsp.
- Butter – ¼ cup
- Pepper – ¼ tsp.
- Garlic powder – ¼ tsp.

Method

1. Brown the beef on Sauté in the Instant Pot.
2. Remove into a bowl. Drain grease and clean the pot.
3. Add water into the pot and place steam rack.
4. Place the bowl with the beef on top.
5. Add garlic powder, pepper, butter, salt, and spinach.
6. Cover with a foil and close the lid.
7. Press Manual and cook 2 minutes on High.
8. Do a quick release.
9. Remove foil, stir and serve.

Nutritional Facts Per Serving

- o   Calories: 272
- o   Fat: 19.1g
- o   Carb: 0.6g
- o   Protein: 18.3g

Chapter 6 Fish and Seafood

Crab Legs with Butter Sauce

Prep time: 3 minutes	Cook time: 7 minutes	Servings: 2

Ingredients

- Crab legs – 2 pounds, rinsed
- Water – 1 cup
- Butter – 4 Tbsps.
- Mince garlic – 1 clove
- Lemon – ½, juiced
- Lemon wedges – 4

Method

1. Add water into the Instant Pot.
2. Place steamer basket and crab legs on top.
3. Close the lid and press Steam.
4. Cook 7 minutes.
5. Do a quick release and remove the crab legs.
6. Mix the butter and lemon juice.

7. Serve crab legs with the sauce and lemon wedges.

Nutritional Facts Per Serving

- o   Calories: 511

- o   Fat: 22.5g

- o   Carb: 1g

- o   Protein: 66.7g

Shrimp and Crab Stew

Prep time: 10 minutes	Cook time: 15 minutes	Servings: 4

Ingredients

- Coconut oil – 1 Tbsp.
- Onion – ½, diced
- Minced garlic – 2 cloves
- Chopped celery – 2 stalks
- Bay leaf – 1
- Old Bay seasoning – 2 tsps.
- Salt – 1 tsp.
- Shrimp - 1 pound, shelled, deveined, and chopped
- Lump crab meat – 1 pound
- Seafood stock – 4 cups
- Butter – 2 Tbsps.
- Heavy cream – ¼ cup

Method

1. Heat the coconut oil on Sauté in the Instant Pot.
2. Add onions and sauté for 3 minutes.
3. Add garlic and sauté for 30 seconds.
4. Press Cancel.
5. Except for the heavy cream, add all remaining ingredients.

6. Close the lid and press Manual.
7. Cook 10 minutes on High.
8. Do a quick release and stir in heavy cream.
9. Serve.

Nutritional Facts Per Serving

o   Calories: 326

o   Fat: 15.4g

o   Carb: 3.2g

o   Protein: 28.3g

Shrimp Stir-Fry

Prep time: 10 minutes	Cook time: 10 minutes	Servings: 4

Ingredients

- Coconut oil – 2 Tbsps.
- Medium shrimp – 1 pound, shelled and deveined
- Button mushrooms – ½ cup
- Diced zucchini – ½ cup
- Broccoli florets – 2 cups
- Liquid aminos – ¼ cup
- Minced garlic – 2 cloves
- Red pepper flakes – 1/8 tsp.
- Cooked cauliflower rice – 2 cups

Method

1. Heat the coconut oil on Sauté in the Instant Pot.
2. Add shrimp and stir-fry until fully cooked, about 5 minutes. Remove and set aside.
3. Add red pepper flakes, garlic, liquid aminos, broccoli, zucchini, and mushrooms. Stir-fry for 3 to 5 minutes.
4. Add shrimp back to pot and press cancel.
5. Serve with cauliflower rice.

Nutritional Facts Per Serving

- Calories: 173

- Fat: 7.4g

- Carb: 7g

- Protein: 19.3g

Buttered Scallops

Prep time: 5 minutes	Cook time: 5 minutes	Servings: 4

Ingredients

- o Avocado oil – 2 Tbsps.
- o Large sea scallops – 1 pound, prepared
- o Salt – 1/8 tsp.
- o Pepper – 1/8 tsp.
- o Melted butter – 2 Tbsp.

Method

1. Press Sauté and heat the avocado oil in the Instant Pot.
2. Season scallops with salt and pepper.
3. Sear scallops 2 to 3 minutes on each side.
4. Pour butter over scallops and serve hot.

Nutritional Facts Per Serving

- o Calories: 190

- o Fat: 12.4g

- ○ Carb: 3.7g
- ○ Protein: 13.7g

Lemon Dill Salmon

Prep time: 3 minutes	Cook time: 5 minutes	Servings: 2

Ingredients

- o   Salmon filets – 2 (3-oz.)
- o   Chopped fresh dill – 1 tsp.
- o   Salt – ½ tsp.
- o   Pepper – ¼ tsp.
- o   Water – 1 cup
- o   Lemon juice – 2 Tbsps.
- o   Lemon – ½, sliced

Method

1. Season the salmon with salt, pepper, and dill.
2. Add water to the Instant Pot and place steam rack.
3. Place salmon on the steam rack (skin side down).
4. Drizzle with lemon juice and put lemon slices on top.
5. Close the lid and press Steam.
6. Cook 5 minutes on High.
7. Do a quick release and serve with lemon slices and dill.

Nutritional Facts Per Serving

- o Calories: 127

- o Fat: 4.9g

- o Carb: 1.5g

- o Protein: 17.1g

Lemon Butter Lobster Tail

Prep time: 5 minutes	Cook time: 4 minutes	Servings: 2

Ingredients

- Chicken broth – 1 cup
- Water – ½ cup
- Old Bay seasoning – 1 tsp.
- Fresh lobster tails – 2 (12-ounce)
- Juice of ½ lemon
- Butter – 2 Tbsps. melted
- Salt – ¼ tsp.
- Dried parsley – ¼ tsp.
- Pepper – 1/8 tsp.

Method

1. Add water, broth, and seasoning into the Instant Pot.
2. Place lobster tails on the steam rack, shell side down.
3. Close the lid and press Manual.
4. Cook 4 minutes on High.
5. Do a quick release.

6. In a bowl, combine salt, pepper, parsley, butter, and lemon juice.
7. Crack open tail and dip into the butter sauce.

Nutritional Facts Per Serving

- o Calories: 259

- o Fat: 17.3g

- o Carb: 1g

- o Protein: 32.9g

Salmon Burger with Avocado

Prep time: 10 minutes	Cook time: 5 minutes	Servings: 4

Ingredients

- Coconut oil - 2 Tbsps.
- Salmon filets – 1 pound, skin removed and finely minced
- Salt – ½ tsp.
- Garlic powder – ¼ tsp.
- Chili powder – ¼ tsp.
- Finely diced onion – 2 Tbsps.
- Egg – 1
- Mayo – 2 Tbsps.
- Ground pork rinds – 1/3 cup
- Avocado – 1, mashed
- Juice of ½ lime

Method

1. Melt the coconut oil on Sauté in the Instant Pot.
2. Place salmon in a bowl.
3. Add remaining ingredients except for lime and avocado.
4. Mix and form 4 patties.

5. Place burgers into the pot and sear 3 to 4 minutes per side.
6. Press Cancel and set aside.
7. Mix lime juice and avocado in a bowl.
8. Divide mash into four sections and place on top of the salmon patties.
9. Serve.

Nutritional Facts Per Serving

- Calories: 425

- Fat: 27.6g

- Carb: 1.3g

- Protein: 35.6g

Foil Pack Salmon

Prep time: 2 minutes	Cook time: 7 minutes	Servings: 2

Ingredients

- Salmon fillets – 2 (3 oz.)
- Salt – 1 tsp.
- Pepper – ¼ tsp.
- Garlic powder – ¼ tsp.
- Dried dill – ¼ tsp.
- Lemon – ½, sliced
- **Water – 1 cup**

Method

1. Place salmon on a square of foil, skin side down.
2. Season with seasoning and drizzle with lemon juice.
3. Place lemon slice on each filet.
4. Pour water in the Instant Pot and place a steam rack.
5. Place foil packets on the steam rack and close the lid.
6. Press Steam and cook 7 minutes.
7. Do a quick release.

8. Serve.

Nutritional Facts Per Serving

- ○   Calories: 125

- ○   Fat: 4.6g

- ○   Carb: 0.4g

- ○   Protein: 18.5g

Almond Pesto Salmon

Prep time: 5 minutes	Cook time: 7 minutes	Servings: 4

Ingredients

- Sliced almonds – ¼ cup
- Butter – 1 Tbsp.
- Salmon fillets – 4 (3-oz.)
- Pesto – ½ cup
- Salt – ½ tsp.
- Pepper – ¼ tsp.
- Water – 1 cup

Method

1. Press Sauté and add butter into the Instant Pot.
2. Sauté almonds for 3 to 5 minutes. Remove and set aside.
3. Season the salmon with salt, pepper, and brush with pesto.
4. Pour water into the Instant Pot and place steam rack.
5. Add salmon to the rack.
6. Close the lid and press Steam.
7. Cook 7 minutes.
8. Serve with almond slices on top.

Nutritional Facts Per Serving

- Calories: 182

- Fat: 20.5g

- Carb: 3g

- Protein: 21.2g

Tomato Cod

Prep time: 5 minutes	Cook time: 15 minutes	Servings: 4

Ingredients

- Butter – 2 Tbsp.
- Diced onion – ¼ cup
- Minced garlic – 1 clove
- Cherry tomatoes – 1 cup, chopped
- Salt – ¼ tsp.
- Pepper – 1/8 tsp.
- Dried thyme – ¼ tsp.
- Chicken broth – ¼ cup
- Capers – 1 Tbsp.
- Cod filets – 4 (4-oz.)
- Water – 1 cup
- Chopped parsley – ¼ cup

Method

1. Melt the butter on Sauté in the instant pot.
2. Add onion and stir-fry until soften.
3. Add garlic and cook 30 seconds more.
4. Add broth, thyme, pepper, salt, and chopped tomatoes.

5. Cook 5 to 7 minutes or until tomatoes soften. Press Cancel.
6. Pour sauce into a bowl.
7. Add fish fillets and capers. Cover with foil.
8. Pour water into the Instant Pot.
9. Place the steam rack on the bottom.
10. Place bowl on top.
11. Close the lid and press Manual.
12. Cook 3 minutes.
13. Do a quick release.
14. Sprinkle with fresh parsley and serve.

Nutritional Facts Per Serving

o Calories: 157

o Fat:7.3g

o Carb: 2.2g

o Protein: 21g

Fish Taco Bowls

Prep time: 15 minutes	Cook time: 5 minutes	Servings: 4

Ingredients

- Shredded cabbage – 4 cups
- Mayo – ¼ cup
- Sour cream – 2 Tbsp.
- Lime – 1, halved
- Chopped pickled jalapenos – 2 Tbsp.
- Tilapia filets – 3 (4-oz.)
- Chili powder – 2 tsp.
- Cumin – 1 tsp.
- Garlic powder – 1 tsp.
- Salt – 1 tsp.
- Coconut oil – 2 Tbsp.
- Avocado – 1, diced
- Chopped cilantro – 4 Tbsp.

Method

1. Mix jalapenos, juice of half lime, sour cream, mayo, and cabbage in a bowl.
2. Cover and keep in the refrigerator for 30 minutes.

168

3. Press Sauté and add coconut oil to the Instant Pot.
4. Season the filets with seasonings.
5. Add filets and sear 2 to 4 minutes on each side.
6. Press Cancel.
7. Chop fish into bite-sized pieces.
8. Divide slaw into four bowls and place fish on top.
9. Add chopped avocado, drizzle with lime juice.
10. Sprinkle with cilantro and serve.

Nutritional Facts Per Serving

o   Calories: 328

o   Fat: 23.8g

o   Carb: 4.2g

o   Protein: 19.4g

Crispy Blackened Salmon

Prep time: 5 minutes	Cook time: 5 minutes	Servings: 2

Ingredients

- o Salmon filets – 2 (3-ounce)
- o Avocado oil – 1 Tbsp.
- o Paprika – 1 tsp.
- o Salt – ½ tsp.
- o Pepper – ¼ tsp.
- o Onion powder – ¼ tsp.
- o Dried thyme – ¼ tsp.
- o Cayenne pepper – 1/8 tsp.

Method

1. Drizzle the salmon with avocado oil.
2. In a bowl, mix remaining ingredients and rub over filets.
3. Press Sauté and place salmon into the Instant Pot.
4. Sear 2 to 5 minutes until seasoning is blackened.
5. Serve.

Nutritional Facts Per Serving

- o Calories: 190

- Fat: 11.4g
- Carb: 1g
- Protein: 18.6g

Steamed Clams

Prep time: 5 minutes	Cook time: 5 minutes	Servings: 4

Ingredients

- Clams – 2 pounds
- Seafood stock – 1 cup
- Butter – 4 Tbsp.

Method

1. Place seafood stock and clams into the Instant Pot.
2. Close the lid.
3. Press Steam and cook 5 minutes.
4. Do a quick release.
5. Serve with butter.

Nutritional Facts Per Serving

- Calories: 151

- Fat: 11g

- Carb: 2.1g

- Protein: 8.7g

Cajun Shrimp, Crab, and Sausage Boil

Prep time: 10 minutes	Cook time: 5 minutes	Servings: 4

Ingredients

- Smoked sausage – ½ pound
- Shelled deveined large shrimp – ½ pound
- Crab legs – 2 pounds
- Seafood stock – 2 cups
- Cajun seasoning – 1 Tbsp.

Method

1. Place all ingredients into the Instant Pot and close the lid.
2. Press Steam and cook 5 minutes.
3. Do a quick release and serve.

Nutritional Facts Per Serving

- Calories: 239

- Fat: 8g

- o Carb: 5.2g

- o Protein: 32.2g

Butter Shrimp with Asparagus

Prep time: 5 minutes	Cook time: 3 minutes	Servings: 2

Ingredients

- Prepared shrimp – 1 pound
- Minced garlic – 1 clove
- Salt – ½ tsp.
- Pepper – ¼ tsp.
- Paprika – ¼ tsp.
- Red pepper flakes – 1/8 tsp.
- Asparagus – ½ pound, cut into bite-sized pieces
- Juice of ½ lemon
- Butter – 4 Tbsp.
- Chopped fresh parsley – 2 tsp.
- Water – 1 cup

Method

1. Sprinkle shrimp with red pepper flakes, paprika, pepper, salt, and garlic.
2. Place in a bowl and add asparagus.
3. Drizzle with lemon juice and mix.

176

4. Place cubed butter around the dish.
5. Sprinkle with parsley and cover with foil.
6. Add water to the Instant Pot and place steam rack.
7. Place the dish on the steam rack and close the lid.
8. Press Steam and cook 3 minutes.
9. Do a quick release.
10. Remove and serve.

Nutritional Facts Per Serving

o   Calories: 381

o   Fat: 23.2g

o   Carb: 4.3g

o   Protein: 32.7g

Chapter 7 Desserts

Crestless Berry Cheesecake

Prep time: 10 minutes	Cook time: 40 minutes	Servings: 12

Ingredients

- o Cream cheese – 16 ounces, softened
- o Powdered erythritol – 1 cup
- o Sour cream – ¼ cup
- o Vanilla extract – 2 tsp.
- o Eggs – 2
- o Water – 2 cups
- o Blackberries and strawberries – ¼ cup, as the topping

Method

1. Beat erythritol and cream cheese until smooth.
2. Add eggs, vanilla, and sour cream and combine.
3. Pour batter into a springform pan.
4. Cover top with tinfoil.

5. Pour water into the Instant Pot and place steam rack in pot.
6. Place the pan on top of the rack.
7. Close and press Cake.
8. Cook 40 minutes and do a natural release when done.
9. Remove and cool.
10. Top with berries and serve.

Nutritional Facts Per Serving

o Calories: 153

o Fat: 12.7g

o Carb: 1.9g

o Protein: 3.4g

Almond Butter Fat Bomb

Prep time: 3 minutes	Cook time: 3 minutes	Servings: 6

Ingredients

- Coconut oil – ¼ cup

- No-sugar-added almond butter – ¼ cup

- Cacao powder – 2 Tbsp.

- Powdered erythritol – ¼ cup

Method

1. Melt the coconut oil on Sauté in the Instant Pot.
2. Press Cancel and stir in remaining ingredients.
3. Pour the mixture into 6 silicone molds.
4. Freeze and serve.

Nutritional Facts Per Serving

- Calories: 142

- Fat: 14.1g

- o Carb: 1.4g

- o Protein: 2g

Chocolate Chip Fat Bomb

Prep time: 2 minutes	Cook time: 2 minutes	Servings: 12

Ingredients

- Coconut oil – ½ cup

- No-sugar-added peanut butter - ½ cup

- Cream cheese – 2 ounces, warmed

- Powdered erythritol – ¼ cup

- Low-carb chocolate chips – ¼ cup

Method

1. Melt coconut oil in the Instant Pot on Sauté.
2. Add erythritol, cream cheese, and peanut butter. Mix.
3. Pour mixture into silicone baking cups.
4. Sprinkle the cups with chocolate chips.
5. Freeze in the freezer and serve.

Nutritional Facts Per Serving

- Calories: 181

- Fat: 16.8g

- o Carb: 3.6g

- o Protein: 3g

Chocolate Mousse

Prep time: 5 minutes	Cook time: 5 minutes	Servings: 4

Ingredients

- Heavy whipping cream – 1 cup
- Gelatin – ½ tsp.
- Erythritol – 1 Tbsp.
- Vanilla extract – 1 tsp.
- Chocolate pudding – 1 cup, no sugar added

Method

1. Place gelatin and heavy cream in a bowl.
2. Add into the Instant Pot on Sauté.
3. Whisk until the gelatin is dissolved.
4. Press Cancel and add vanilla and erythritol.
5. Whisk until soft peaks form.
6. Gently fold in chocolate pudding.
7. Serve chilled.

Nutritional Facts Per Serving

- o   Calories: 289

- o   Fat: 23.2g

- o   Carb: 8g

- o   Protein: 2.7g

Blackberry Crunch

Prep time: 5 minutes	Cook time: 5 minutes	Servings: 1

Ingredients

- Blackberries – 10
- Vanilla extract – ½ tsp.
- Powdered erythritol – 2 Tbsp.
- Xanthan gum – 1/8 tsp.
- Butter – 1 Tbsp.
- Chopped pecans – ¼ cup
- Almond flour – 3 tsp.
- Cinnamon – ½ tsp.
- Powdered erythritol – 2 tsp.
- Water – 1 cup

Method

1. Place xanthan gum, erythritol, vanilla, and blackberries in a 4-inch ramekin.
2. Stir to coat the blackberries.
3. Mix remaining ingredients in another bowl.
4. Sprinkle over blackberries and cover with foil.
5. Press Manual and cook 4 minutes.
6. Do a quick release and serve.

Nutritional Facts Per Serving

o Calories: 346

o Fat: 30.7g

o Carb: 5.5g

o Protein: 3.4g

Peanut Butter Cheesecake Bites

Prep time: 10 minutes	Cook time: 15 minutes	Servings: 8

Ingredients

- Cream cheese – 16 oz. softened
- Powdered erythritol – 1 cup
- Peanut flour – ½ cup
- Sour cream – ¼ cup
- Vanilla extract – 2 tsps.
- Eggs – 2
- Water – 2 cups
- Low-carb chocolate chips – ¼ cup
- Coconut oil – 1 Tbsp.

Method

1. Beat erythritol and cream cheese until smooth in a bowl.
2. Gently fold in sour cream, flour, and vanilla. Fold in eggs until mixed.
3. Pour batter into silicone cupcake molds or 4-inch springform pans.
4. Cover with foil and pour water into the Instant Pot.
5. Place steam rack in the pot and add foil covered pan on top.
6. Close the lid and press Cake.
7. Cook 15 minutes.
8. Do a natural release. Remove and cool.
9. Add coconut oil and chocolate chips in a bowl.
10. Melt in the microwave for 30 seconds and whisk until smooth.
11. Drizzle over cheesecakes.
12. Chill and serve.

Nutritional Facts Per Serving

o   Calories: 290

o   Fat: 22.8g

o   Carb: 6.5g

o   Protein: 7g

Pecan Clusters

Prep time: 5 minutes	Cook time: 5 minutes	Servings: 8

Ingredients

- Butter – 3 Tbsp.
- Heavy cream – ¼ cup
- Vanilla extract – 1 tsp.
- Chopped pecans – 1 cup
- Low-carb chocolate chips – ¼ cup

Method

1. Melt the butter on Sauté in the Instant Pot.
2. Once the butter is brown, add heavy cream and press Cancel.
3. Add chopped pecans and vanilla.
4. Cool and stir occasionally for 10 minutes.
5. Line a baking sheet with parchment and spoon mixture on it to form eight clusters.

6. Scatter chocolate chips over clusters.
7. Cool and serve.

Nutritional Facts Per Serving

o   Calories: 194

o   Fat: 18.2g

o   Carb: 4g

o   Protein: 1.5g

Classic Fudge

Prep time: 5 minutes	Cook time: 3 minutes	Servings: 10

Ingredients

- Low-carb chocolate chips – 1 cup
- Cream cheese – 8 ounces
- Erythritol – ¼ cup
- Cinnamon – ¼ tsp.
- Vanilla extract – 1 tsp.
- Water – 1 cup

Method

1. Place vanilla, cinnamon, erythritol, cream cheese, and chocolate chips on a bowl. Cover with foil.
2. Pour water in the Instant Pot and place steam rack.
3. Place the bowl on the rack and cover the lid.
4. Press Manual and cook for 3 minutes.
5. Do a natural release.
6. Remove bowl carefully and stir until smooth.
7. Line a pan with parchment paper and pour mixture on it.

8. Chill, slice, and serve.

Nutritional Facts Per Serving

- o Calories: 190

- o Fat: 13.9g

- o Carb: 9g

- o Protein: 1.4g

Lemon Poppy Seed Cake

Prep time: 10 minutes	Cook time: 25 minutes	Servings: 6

Ingredients

- Almond flour – 1 cup
- Eggs – 2
- Erythritol – ½ cup
- Vanilla extract – 2 tsp.
- Lemon extract – 1 tsp.
- Poppy seeds – 1 Tbsp.
- Melted butter – 4 Tbsp.
- Heavy cream – ¼ cup
- Sour cream – 1/8 cup
- Baking powder – ½ tsp.
- Water – 1 cup
- Powdered erythritol – ¼ cup, for garnish

Method

1. In a bowl, mix poppy seeds, lemon, vanilla, erythritol, eggs, and almond flour.
2. Add baking powder, sour cream, heavy cream, and butter.
3. Pour into 7-inch round cake pan and cover with foil.
4. Pour the water into the Instant Pot and place a steam rack.
5. Place the cake pan on top of the rack.
6. Close the lid and press Cake.
7. Cook 25 minutes.
8. Do a natural release.
9. Cool and sprinkle with powdered erythritol.
10. Serve.

Nutritional Facts Per Serving

o   Calories: 240

o   Fat: 20.8g

o   Carb: 3g

o   Protein: 2.7g

Brownies

Prep time: 15 minutes	Cook time: 25 minutes	Servings: 6

Ingredients

- Low-carb chocolate chips – 1 cup

- Coconut oil – 1 Tbsp.

- Cream cheese – 1 oz. warmed

- Heavy cream – ¼ cup

- Almond flour – 1 cup

- Eggs – 2

- Baking soda – ½ tsp.

- Melted butter – 4 Tbsp.

- Powdered erythritol – ¾ cup

- Gelatin – 1 tsp.

- Cocoa powder – ½ cup

- Water – 1 cup

196

Method

1. Melt coconut oil and chocolate chips in the microwave. Whisk until smooth. Set aside.
2. In another bowl, mix cocoa powder, gelatin, erythritol, butter, baking soda, eggs, almond flour, heavy cream, and cream cheese. Fold in melted chocolate.
3. Pour mixture into 7-inch round cake pan and cover with foil.
4. Pour water into the Instant Pot and place steam rack.
5. Place pan on the steam rack and close the lid.
6. Press manual adds cook for 25 minutes.
7. Do a natural release and serve.

Nutritional Facts Per Serving

o   Calories: 460

o   Fat: 35.9g

o   Carb: 11g

o   Protein: 5.1g

Peanut Butter Fudge

Prep time: 5 minutes	Cook time: 2 hours	Servings: 12

Ingredients

- Low-carb chocolate chips – 1 cup
- Cream cheese – 8 oz.
- Erythritol – ¼ cup
- No-sugar-added peanut butter – ¼ cup
- Vanilla extract – 1 tsp.

Method

1. Add all the ingredients and cover with slow cooker lid.
2. Cook on low for 1 hour and stir.
3. Smooth mixture and cook for 30 minutes more.
4. Line a pan with parchment and pour mixture on it.
5. Chill and serve.

Nutritional Facts Per Serving

- Calories: 159
- Fat: 11.5g

- Carb: 9.5g
- Protein: 1.9g

Chocolate Pudding

Prep time: 5 minutes	Cook time: 15 minutes	Servings: 4

Ingredients

- Vanilla almond milk – 2 cups, unsweetened, and divided
- Heavy cream – ½ cup
- Egg yolks – 2
- Vanilla extract – 1 tsp.
- Cinnamon – 1/8 tsp.
- Cocoa powder - 2 Tbsps.
- Guar gum – ¾ tsp.
- Low-carb chocolate chips – ¼ cup

Method

1. Press Sauté and add half of the almond milk and heavy cream into the Instant Pot.

2. Bring to a gentle boil.
3. In a bowl, add guar gum, cocoa powder, cinnamon, vanilla, and yolks and whisk to mix.
4. Slowly whisk this mixture into the Instant Pot mixture. Mix until smooth.
5. Press Cancel and add chocolate chips.
6. Whisk until melted.
7. Pour mixture into a large bowl and refrigerate for 2 hours.
8. Serve.

Nutritional Facts Per Serving

o   Calories: 224

o   Fat: 18.7g

o   Carb: 8g

o   Protein: 3g

Chocolate Cheesecake

Prep time: 10 minutes	Cook time: 50 minutes	Servings: 12

Ingredients

- Pecans – 2 cups
- Butter – 2 Tbsps.
- Cream cheese – 16 ounces, softened
- Erythritol – 1 cup, powdered
- Sour cream – ¼ cup
- Cocoa powder – 2 Tbsps.
- Vanilla extract – 2 tsps.
- Low-carb chocolate chips – 2 cups
- Eggs – 2
- Coconut oil – 1 Tbsp

o   Water – 2 cups

Method

1. Preheat oven to 400F.
2. Pulse butter and pecan in a food processor until dough like consistency.
3. Press into bottom of 7-inch springform pan.
4. Bake for 10 minutes, remove and cool.
5. Meanwhile, in a bowl, add vanilla, cocoa powder, sour cream, erythritol, and cream cheese. Mix and set aside.
6. In another bowl, combine coconut oil and chocolate chips.
7. Melt in the microwave then stir until smooth.
8. Gently fold the chocolate mixture into the cheesecake mixture.
9. Gently fold in the eggs. Do not overmix.
10. Pour mixture over cooled pecan crust and cover with foil.
11. Pour water into the Instant Pot and place the steam rack.
12. Place the cake pan on the rack and close the lid.
13. Press Manual and cook for 40 minutes.
14. Do a natural release.
15. Cool and serve.

Nutritional Facts Per Serving

o   Calories: 481

o   Fat: 38.9g

o   Carb: 9.3g

- Protein: 5.1g

Chocolate Mug Cake

Prep time: 5 minutes	Cook time: 20 minutes	Servings: 1

Ingredients

o   Water – 1 cup

o   Almond flour – ¼ cup

o   Coconut flour – 2 Tbsps.

o   Egg – 1

o   Erythritol – 2 Tbsps.

o   Vanilla extract – ½ tsp.

o   Butter – 1 Tbsp.

o   Cocoa powder – 2 tsps.

Method

1. Pour water into the Instant pot and place the steam rack.
2. Mix remaining ingredients and mix in a mug. Cover with foil.
3. Place the mug onto steam rack and close the lid.
4. Press Manual and cook for 20 minutes.

5. Do a natural release.
6. Serve.

Nutritional Facts Per Serving

- Calories: 384

- Fat: 28.5g

- Carb: 7.4

- Protein: 9.1g

Vanilla Tea Cake

Prep time: 10 minutes	Cook time: 25 minutes	Servings: 8

Ingredients

- o   Almond flour – 1 cup
- o   Eggs – 2
- o   Erythritol – ½ cup
- o   Vanilla extract – 2 tsps.
- o   Melted butter – 4 Tbsps.
- o   Heavy cream – ¼ cup
- o   Baking powder – ½ tsp.
- o   Water – 1 cup

Method

1. In a bowl, mix all ingredients except water.
2. Pour into a round cake pan.
3. Cover with foil.
4. Add water into the Instant Pot and place the steam rack.

5. Place baking pan on the rack and close the lid.
6. Press Cake and cook for 25 minutes.
7. Do a natural release.
8. Cool and serve.

Nutritional Facts Per Serving

- Calories: 166

- Fat: 14.6g

- Carb: 8g

- Protein: 1.8g

Conclusion

Thanks to the Instant Pot, eating keto has never been easier. By using these quick, healthy, and delicious Instant Pot recipes, you will realize that home-cooked keto meals do not have to be time-consuming or challenging. If you are looking for a proper guide for every kind of food that you can cook in your Instant Pot, you should have these recipes in your collection. Not only do the recipes included in this book fit within the ketogenic diet, but they are incredibly easy to prepare.

Made in the USA
Middletown, DE
18 December 2019